WALKING NAKED
WITH THE LORD

WALKING NAKED
WITH THE LORD

*a contemporary look at the winners
and losers in God's Holy Book*

JUDITH ANNE RUSSETT

XULON PRESS

Xulon Press
2301 Lucien Way #415
Maitland, FL 32751
407.339.4217
www.xulonpress.com

Unless otherwise indicated, Scripture quotations taken from the New King James Version (NKJV). Copyright © 1982 by Thomas Nelson, Inc. Used by permission. All rights reserved.

Edited by Xulon Press

Printed in the United States of America.

ISBN-13: 978-1-54566-761-3

TABLE OF CONTENTS

PREFACE

enesis tells us of a first consequence the day Adam and Eve fell from grace in the Garden of Eden: it was in the sudden awareness of being "naked."

We are told this realization translated quickly into feelings of deep shame. The first thing Adam and Eve did was to harvest some fig leaves to conceal their physical exposure and to hide themselves from their heavenly Father's anticipated displeasure.

Instinctively they knew that single act of disobedience committed in defiance of the Father's will compromised their once perfect existence in the Garden of Eden. Paradise, where all had existed in harmony and perfect balance, suddenly morphed into a dangerous, unknown, damaged place. Most terrifying of all, the intimate relationship with their Creator was irreparably broken. Their cries for his forgiveness went unanswered.

The consequences for Adam and Eve were harsh, and God's justice followed swiftly. Their actions exiled them into a world of unfamiliar changes. All the natural beauty around them remained, but the colors were dimmer, the shadows darker. Even the animals appeared threatening.

The knowledge they had coveted and paid dearly to acquire was now fused into a permanent unpalatable reality.

You would expect that all Believers who came after would never forget the lessons learned in that time. Instead, history shows selfish choices were destined to become a telling characteristic of the human condition. As the story unfolds, the Old Testament spends the first half of the Bible relating the tales of God's foolish people, who continued to make reckless decisions outside of his laws. *Apparently human beings were, and still are, slow learners.*

Even so, the Father promised a "land of milk and honey" and a Savior to destroy the barriers of sin that separated his people from his loving embrace. He gave mankind a second chance with the promise of redemption. That day would be long in coming. The Father would require man be tested again for his commitment to God's ways first.

Unfortunately, true to form, human beings proved to be ungrateful for the blessings that had been bestowed upon them. Man continued to pursue a relentless path of self-destruction and disobedience. The same self-seeking human priorities that marked our species from the beginning of time—when we thought what we had was not enough the first time—remained evident in the stories of the forty years spent wandering the desert.

Since then human beings have become, if possible, more adept at rationalizing their actions, or lack thereof. Even after the promised Savior's arrival, we are not unlike those ancient men and women who couldn't wait to turn back to their pagan ways when Moses left for Mount Tabor at the calling of his Lord.

Like them, we continue to fall back on worshipping the same idols of old, wearing the same fig leaves of denial and rationalization to hide our shame. One key difference: since that first sin in the Garden, the selection of fig leaves has grown into an entire wardrobe!

How do we as struggling Christians find our way out of the maze that surrounds us? How can we divest ourselves of the fig leaves we've come to rely on when the world around us has adopted a uniform of the same?

We can turn to God's book, the Bible.

Constantly revealing, the Bible has themes underneath the basic story lines that can be easily overlooked. While the content is full of those who fell from grace and suffered the consequences, maybe there is more to learn than the obvious lessons of retribution and suffering that befell these unfortunate souls. Since the Holy Book has no extraneous material, the "losers"—so to speak—who so generously pepper its pages must be necessary reading material for a reason. P*erhaps we are them, and they are us?*

Certainly, we have the same basic needs, fears, and desires as our predecessors. We face the same struggles on our journey to acceptance of God's ways. Our actions are rationalized with the same feeble excuses and explana-tions when we attempt to find our way around the Father's will. While we count ourselves lucky not to be one of the most reviled (e.g., Pontius Pilate, the innkeeper, Judas and so many others whose names have gone down in infamy), it can become easy to measure their trespasses against our own with a sense of relief.

Perhaps we need to look more deeply into these controversial souls?

This book is about doing just that. We are going to take a hard look at some of the winners and losers in the Bible. We'll do it by stripping to the basics and peeking under the proverbial fig leaves to expose the truth between God and Man: *every person we read about is a story ongoing in our own times.*

Now as then, there is nothing God does not see. There is no hiding the worst of ourselves, no cloaking our intentions or actions in ambiguity, no keeping the secret, dark, and shameful intent of our hearts from him.

With that in mind, I have taken the liberty of assigning personalities to some of the people in the Bible. I will be examining the "fig leaves" they may have worn to disguise and defend their failings from God. I will also try to show that even those who willingly chose his ways often paid prices we seldom think about. I do this in the hope each of us might recognize in the recounting of their stories the striking similarities to our own modern trespasses. Perhaps we will be motivated to come to the Father with new humility—and certainly a new wardrobe.

The Bible is about winners and losers, about man's inhumanity to man. It's about fallible human beings and God's love for them all.

It's about *you* and *me.*

And the Lord said:
"My heart is an open book."

"Come,
I will teach you to Read."

DESTROYER OF LIGHT

The name you call me by is not really mine. Certainly, you have assigned enough of them to me throughout the ages. The images of me are varied as well. It doesn't matter what you call me by or what I may appear as. *You know me.*

I was created from the same Universal Energy you were. Did you humans really think you were the best the Creator could do? It didn't occur to you the Almighty might have produced others more gifted? It would prove typical of your arrogant ways.

When your Father and mine acted as Creator, he poured his energy into those he would first surround his throne with. It wasn't you or your kind. Before the Father created human beings, he brought us into being. We shared in an eternal Communion with him. Pure spirit, our sole purpose and desire was to praise his Holy Name. We were perfect and perfectly content in ways later man could not hope to match.

Then one day, he brought you forth and things changed.

I wasn't the only one who couldn't understand it. It was obvious from the get-go you fragile humans were nothing like us. You didn't have our beauty, our gifts or our grace, yet the

1

Father created you in his own image. When we found out he had bestowed free will on you, we were astonished.

I, for one, was angry. Had he lost all sense? Why should you be exalted over us? I tried to reason with him. I suggested it was dangerous to allow you weak human creatures to choose your own way. Since I held great favor in his eyes, I'd hoped that he would hear me. Clearly, he was enamored of you; in love with the very contradictions in your nature I and others saw as worrisome. We, once his favored, were but white noise.

He did not even demand your love in acknowledgement of his gifts, but would have you choose to return it willingly. He plainly was not in control. The next thing we knew, we'd be serving as messengers and guides to you! It was too much to bear.

With a haughty, angry spirit, I challenged the Almighty's leadership. It didn't occur to me at the time no created creature could ever be greater than the Source from whence he came. I was simply beside myself. On the day I became that superior person in my own mind, I lost my connection to the Father's inner circle. It happened in an instant.

Did he cast me out, or did I become an outcast because I no longer shone with the Light of the Almighty? Cast into darkness from the Light by virtue of the sin of pride?

It mattered little. In my mind you human beings were responsible for my loss. I set myself this task: I would prove just how worthless and easily corrupted you were. It would become my life's work. That first successful challenge that played out in the Garden of Eden was confirmation of my power and my destiny.

Since then I have exploited every human weakness to encourage your failings. I will continue to do battle with the Father for your souls until the end of time. He allows it after all. It's still about that "free will" he gave you. As for me, I'm grateful you have it. I can encourage the use of it to my advantage.

Every choice you make in my favor strips you a little of his light and takes you further away from that eternal communion it pains me every day to have lost. Count on this: I will do all the damage I can. I will take as many of you with me as possible. That is what this war is about. Deny my existence. That too works for me.

You know me as Lucifer, the Dark Angel, Satan, the Devil, Evil Incarnate, the Great Deceiver, the Master of Lies.

Call me whoever you want, speak my name in any tongue that pleases you. Call me by none. I am with you, regardless. Until the end of days.

When the trumpet sounds, I will be there to collect my bounty. You will belong to me.

CONTEMPLATION

Some say the Devil doesn't exist. When applying any of the human senses we rely on to define our normal reality, they would appear to be right: he isn't here. Using the same criteria, some would reason, then, neither is God.

Yet, there are many things in our world outside of our human sensory levels that are no less real for our lack of understanding. The atom, the building block of matter, was always there. Thousands of planets were in orbit all around us while only nine inhabited our reality for centuries. They didn't need our acknowledgment to exist until we discovered them.

Science itself is the discovery of an invisible order that already exists. Man didn't create it. Being ignorant of its presence has not proven to have any bearing on the truth. Not believing clearly does not negate the reality, either.

Which brings us to Satan. While he operates outside our human limitations, we can sense him around us more than we care to admit; especially when he presents himself as our ally in rationalizing why we should have what we want. He's usually going where we want to go.

Being invisible works for him. Our desires are harder to deny when the enemy isn't around in a form we can relate to. It's easier to dismiss the whole idea of temptation as our own invention, to set it aside when it challenges our choices. The devil's happy to go along. He's motivated by a loss he can never recover from. He is focused on inflicting the same on us.

When Lucifer's traitorous thoughts first took root, they were incompatible with the Creator's divine energy. Like two magnets repelling one another, the all-positive energy of the Almighty could not exist in the same space as the negative energy that Lucifer's actions created. *Our own universal laws confirm the same: for every action, there is an equal and opposite reaction.* Lucifer found himself outside the place of pure light and cast into the "opposite realm" of eternal darkness. Paradise was no longer available to him. The unbearable thought that man can still claim that perfect place with the Father fills him with rage and a consuming need for revenge.

He seeks to own the very souls of men by destroying the Light of the Creator that shines in them. He does this by encouraging choices for the darkness. He has learned well since the Garden how to use our human natures against us in pursuit of that goal.

Like any experienced hunter, he is clever. He uses the weakness of his prey to draw his quarry in. We, like all living creatures, only run from the hunter if we perceive the danger. If the temptation is appealing enough, we my disregard our misgivings altogether. Much of the time his offerings seem innocent enough. *Good bait always does.*

The tempting assortment he lays before us consistently has to do with our getting what we already desire. Fortunately for him, we don't like to deny ourselves much. Sadly, man does not realize the collective damage of his self-indulgent ways. All those choices add up over a lifetime, and with enough darkness, the Father's light in us can be gradually overcome and even extinguished.

INTERCESSION

Lord, to be human is to have weaknesses. Since the loss of Eden, we are of a contradictory nature. We battle on the one hand with our physical desires, vulnerable to instant gratification. On the other, we struggle to have the patience to resist temptation while we wait for your return, just as our forefathers did.

While eternal damnation should be a strong deterrent, our own death often seems far removed. Life's temptations are so much more rewarding in the moment. *It could be suggested that as a species, we are all nearsighted, by nature and desire.* Satan knows how to play this conflicted nature of ours well.

Help us, Father, to remember that while you are all about love and forgiveness, you are a just God also. Your Holy Book features many stories of the faithful who fell from grace, straying from the intent of your laws and suffering the consequences of your punishments. They are featured for a reason: to remind us that your perfect justice prevails as strongly as your perfect love when we defy your will.

Help us to keep our vision 20/20.

Matthew 7:21 *Not everyone who says to Me, "Lord, Lord," will enter the kingdom of heaven, but only he who does the will of My Father in heaven.*

THE LOST GARDEN

*M*an's history begins with God the Father in a garden created just for us. The Bible tells us we walked with him and talked with him there without effort. Everywhere was indescribable beauty, peace, and harmony. Man, and his mate, wanted for nothing. Only when they began to suspect there was more to be had did they contemplate ignoring the singular request their loving Father had made of them. The Tree of Knowledge, which they had been warned was not for them, became the focus of the first epic struggle.

Jealous by nature, the vengeful spirit of the Lost Angel began his clever campaign there. He planted a seed in the form of a seductive suggestion in Eve's heart: was the Father perhaps keeping the best for himself? Once Eve allowed that thought to take root, the sibilant whispers of the Tempter continued to nurture the fledgling seed into feelings of entitlement. All kinds of possibilities about the tree and its secrets grew, and the desire to possess its power increased in proportion. Whatever the fruit of the tree offered, Eve became convinced that she and Adam could benefit from it. Soon the perceived indignity of being left out reached proportions of self-justification and blossomed into action. *All of this came to be because the first tendril of evil was permitted to take root.*

The price of this first successful temptation was the loss of Eden and the easy relationship with the Creator. The knowledge paid for that truth? "Life Interrupted."

The Father had bestowed the gift of free will, and he remained true to his gift. Man chose to leave the positive energy of the Father with a negative decision that was not compatible with the Source. He cast himself out of God's perfect garden and was forced to live in a purely human world; one without the Father's presence and protection.

The Father knew the suffering of his children and their regret. Like any loving Father, he sought to heal the breech, hoping the lesson had been learned. He offered hope, promising a Savior who would do what was necessary to create a bridge between man and God. As First Parent to Adam and Eve, and like many other parents who would come after, he would still require confirmation of those better intentions from his difficult progeny. It took time, and the Bible is witness to his being sorely disappointed more often than not.

In time he sent his only Son, Jesus, into the imperfect and unbalanced earth garden created of Adam and Eve's folly. There, Jesus would suffer all the injustices, pain, and prejudices that human beings were capable of inflicting.

He set down this story in his book, the Bible. Every word in it records the journey and the consequences of human choices. It orates the clear intentions of a loving father, teacher, parent, and protector. *It demonstrates that the struggles of our forefathers to reach God's glory were much the same as they are today.*

CONTEMPLATION

God the Father brought life into his Universe. He did not work in half measures. His Spirit flowed uninhibited into Creation. Pouring of himself, he called into being everything that was, that is, that forever will be with his Word. He then blessed the Earth with all manner of rich plant and animal life and beauty unsurpassed. To enjoy this bountiful oasis, he populated it with his greatest creation of all: mankind. Bestowing his own likeness, a Pure Light Energy, into these unique creatures would for all eternity identify his children as his own. Still he would not force his love on humankind. By his very nature, he could not.

The ability to choose was his greatest gift. Undoubtedly the Father probably knew that one day the tie that bound his children to him would be tested. He hoped he had prepared them for the battles they would face. He knew the Adversary that waited in the wings was formidable.

INTERCESSION

Adam and Eve failed you, Father. First your Beloved Angel and then your created human beings fell from your grace. Would I have done any better?

Am I not the same as they? Have I not failed you repeatedly in my own time? We human beings are a sorry lot. Yet clearly you see something beautiful in us, something that was born of your own eternal love. Your Light Energy brands us as one of your own.

The world I live in is full of torments and temptations, just as it was in days of old. I struggle against the same Ancient Enemy who is anxious to claim my soul. The difference is I know Jesus has paid the debt for my sins and that he has defeated death itself. The difference is I am blessed to have his Book and his Word to give me the courage and the grace to follow the path laid down to eternal life.

One day I will be with you, Father. The price for my salvation has been paid! I rejoice in that blessing. I give thanks and praise to the Father and the Son and the Holy Spirit who brought me to this Holy Place of Faith.

> **John 2:15–16** *Stop loving this evil world and all that it offers you, for when you love these things you show that you do not really love God.*

THE ALPHA MALE

His name was Adam.

Up to then, he'd had no name, no need of one. He'd never thought about clothing before or experienced the gnawing hunger that assailed him at present. Emotions like shame, discomfort, fear and despair were unknown to him. All were lacks that never existed in his world. He was in torment now, though, panic overtaking him everywhere he turned. Bereft of peace and joy, it was clear his world had been hopelessly altered.

He shouldn't have listened to Eve. It didn't really seem fair, though. The Father had created her for him. He was enamored of her and found it difficult to refuse her anything. More than once, he'd denied her. She just kept at him. Driven and possessed by the fruit of that magnificent tree, she couldn't let it go.

The Father had made it clear the Tree of Knowledge was strictly off limits. Adam had seen no need for more than they already had. Every necessity and desire were met with overwhelming love and indulgence by the Father—even before it could be recognized as such. The beneficent presence of their Father was always there, surrounding them with peace. They

11

would walk and talk in his Garden, alive in joy and contentment and the comfort of the Creator's unconditional love.

What more could the Tree have offered? How was he to know that too much knowledge would be a dangerous thing? That Eve's obsession would awaken them both to the contrary sides of nature?

Where once the beasts of the forest were as fond pets to them, now clearly, they had been shielded from the savagery that was the compliment of their makeup. Their endlessly perfect days were suddenly rife with uncomfortable changes that left them miserable, wet, cold, and afraid. Thunder and lightning had them cowering and begging for their Father's protection. They were mortified and hiding their shame in the bushes, embarrassed by their nudity, unable to imagine walking naked in the garden with the Lord.

Never had they known concerns like these before. Adam had called to the Father for what seemed forever, until he was hoarse and weak with the effort, but still there was no answer from on high. In his heart, there was a dead zone. This overwhelming loss of connection to his Father was the worst of it. The Garden was the same, but forever different; defiled and transformed by shadows and fearsome things that had no place there before the Tree of Knowledge imparted its horrible truth.

How could he have been so foolish? Why could Eve not have been satisfied with all they had? Their disobedience to the Father's will had unleashed nothing but horror and dismissal. Had it been a test? If so, they had failed miserably. All he knew was now he trembled in a once familiar land.

CONTEMPLATION

First man. What or who was Adam before he was first man? Before he had need of a name? Was he a spirit-man, created from the essence of his Father? If so, then that energy was solely positive; there could be no negativity in the Father's sharing of himself. As Creator, the Father held all in perfect balance and harmony. Imagine a world where no negativity of any kind existed, where no knowledge of such a thing was to be had!

So why, then, did the Father create the dilemma with that tree in the first place? Why did he even bring it up if only to make it off limits? Wasn't that what started the whole mess in the first place? Why not leave well enough alone?

Perhaps it's not so hard to understand from a parent's viewpoint. When an infant is born into the world, he is blissfully ignorant of anything that contradicts his needs. To him, his world is much like the Garden of Eden was for Adam and Eve, with every need and desire anticipated and met with unconditional love. He is an open vessel that absorbs comfort, warmth, and sustenance; unaware he is even a separate person.

Of course, parents know that early innocence won't last. Their job is to guide and protect their child as he grows into his own independent person. Teaching obedience, they set limits. Yet, just as with Adam and Eve, it doesn't take long for the testing to begin. By age two, the days of easy compliance are already done. *"No" seems to be an early part of our learning curve as human beings.*

13

When you tell a young child not to touch a hot stove, the first time he forgets or chooses to do so despite the warnings, he develops an acute awareness there are painful consequences in his once perfect world. That day, his personal Eden becomes a new place. It can and will hurt him—especially in disobedience.

No matter how much you love them, as a parent, you can't protect your children forever. Sooner or later, you have to let them go their own way. While you hope the training you've given them will stand them well in their choices, it isn't uncommon for parents to be hurt and even pushed aside in the process of finding independence. Your prayer is one day, seasoned in life and wiser with experience, they will come home and give their love freely back to you.

In truth, our Creator was "First Parent" to Adam and Eve. He gifted his children with free will. He knew that gift would mean nothing if man was never to have the opportunity to use it—and that a formidable adversary was simply biding time to provide the experience. While he tried to protect them with a stern warning, they made a foolish choice despite those efforts.

There were serious consequences for Adam and Eve for their disobedience. More than that, their actions would have far-reaching consequences for all mankind. Their sin altered the inherent balance of the Father's Creation. The negative energy that resulted from their selfish choice was simply not compatible with the purely positive energy of their beloved Father. Where there was light, now there was darkness. Where there was once security, now there was fear.

Where once there had existed a perfect synergy between Father and child, a perfect Garden of Eden, now there was only estrangement.

God remained perfect; man became a flawed human being living in a negatively charged world.

INTERCESSION

I understand, Lord, that when Adam and Eve disobeyed, they disturbed the balance of your perfect creation. While they were still made in your image, they were fully human now, with all the failings and weaknesses of human beings. Even after this grievous betrayal by man, you still chose in your infinite mercy to send your only son, Jesus, to restore the balance of Creation and to bring your wayward children home.

Jesus was the supreme death sacrifice. Being both man and God, he alone could mend the gulf between us. He alone could take all sin upon himself and triumph over death. There was only one condition for us to share in his eternal life: we must claim our salvation and live our lives in obedience to his Father's will.

Obedience is hard for humans. The Devil plays upon that weakness, thwarting our best intentions with things hardest for us to deny ourselves, continually enticing us to break God's laws to satisfy our own desires. Each time we succumb to sin, we lose a little of the light that marks us as one of the Father's own. If we lose enough of that light over a lifetime of poor choices, darkness will overwhelm us and mark us as someone who belongs to the Prince of Darkness instead.

I praise you, Father. I am so grateful for the tremendous sacrifice your Son made to give me this second chance. Grant me the grace and discernment of your Holy Spirit in those moments of temptation that I may triumph over my weak flesh and come to you filled with your light. There the glory of your Garden will once again be restored, and our souls will know the harmony of your everlasting love for all time.

> *James 1:13–14 When tempted no one should say "God is tempting me." For God cannot be tempted by evil, nor does he tempt anyone; but each person is tempted when they are dragged away by their own evil desire and enticed.*

THE FIRST LADY

What had she done?

What was to become of her?

Her once familiar garden was an alien thing to her now. It was hard to believe that only a short time ago it was her only world, and the people in it her only family. In some ways, it looked the same, but in more important ways, nothing existed as it once was. It was as though her eyes had been opened to terrible vistas, and her garden turned into a travesty of itself. Father was angry and silent, and she no longer had that inner sense of his constant presence. The absence of his warmth and protection was unbearable.

Eve had never seen this side of Father before. He had never been anything but indulgent to her every whim. She could not even conceive of him any other way, until she ate of the Fruit of his Garden. Now he had cast both of them out. How could he have done that? They had pleaded unceasingly, but their entreaties fell on deaf ears.

Poor Adam. She had insisted he take the apple. He had not really wanted to, but she wouldn't listen. Now they would both pay a high price for her willfulness and disobedience. It wasn't Father's fault, either. He could have refused to let their choice stand, but he did not. Free will was theirs to exercise. He had taught them that from the beginning.

This sense of abandonment was a terrible thing; a constant, deep, aching pain that gave no rest. Other new sensations like cold, hunger, and shame assailed her. She and Adam were sorely afraid and strangely empty, unable to comfort even each other.

It wasn't like she hadn't tried to deny her longing. That tree—the vision of that beautiful tree—had haunted her thoughts day and night. She was driven by the need to taste the perfect fruit. It was that serpent. That wily, ingratiating snake had played on her desire and curiosity. Where had he come from? Where had he gone?

She knew with the first bite that Father knew. The knowledge of the tree burst painfully over her with the first forbidden taste. Into her came a new and fearful consciousness. She cowered from it, ran from it—but there was no escape.

Everywhere she looked, there was a revelation. Hidden dangers, dark shadows, and menacing sounds bedeviled her with persistent terror. There were shadowy things tracking her in the dark. Even her body was a stranger to her. She felt an urgent need to cover herself.

She would have her ignorance back if she could, but realized with a sinking heart that knowledge cannot be undone. It becomes a living thing, alive in the sharing and in the taking. It was too late now. *The fruit of The Tree of Knowledge was "full awareness".*

There was no going back.

CONTEMPLATION

Free Will. There are those who say there is no such thing, that we are puppets in a plan that has no regard for our choices and that is already preordained outside ourselves. Sometimes it's easy to wonder if that isn't the truth. We try to make good choices, but the world can seem determined to have its own way. We try to make good decisions for those we are responsible for, but again, it can feel like we have little or no impact.

Children have minds of their own from birth. They feel free to exercise their wills just fine. An infant will refuse and wail if the formula isn't to his liking. Two-year olds' have a favorite word: "No!" Teenagers have the same favorite word. They take for granted the right to have their needs and desires met. As adults, we learn there are consequences for our choices.

As we mature, we expect punishment for our poor decisions. A tendency to see our "Godly" actions as fair barter in return for tangible blessings here on earth quickly follows. Before long we become aware of an odd contradiction in that expectation. Sometimes it's like the adage, "no good deed goes unpunished." *Maybe that's because making the choices we are called to make cannot be done with a mind bent on equal returns?*

How many times do we chose the right path and exercise our will to stay firmly on track, only to find ourselves defeated instead of rewarded for our efforts?

Tell me, Lord, how practicing "free will" works when I've given all my best for so many years, but my son chooses meth, or my daughter is addicted to alcohol? Tell me why, when I choose to lose these forty extra pounds that I'm carrying, my will fails me. Explain to me how I can choose with determination to stop my smoking, or to stop my cheating, or my stealing, or my gambling, or my lying, only to find that I am too weak to persevere? How much harder it is to remain committed to the even greater expectations of you, my heavenly Father! Could it be that choosing isn't the same thing as exercising my will?

Maybe one is the intention, while the other is the vehicle for becoming? Choosing is easy. Will power is hard. Our choices don't really come to reality until our will sustains them.

We human beings make good choices more often than we use our will power to see them through. We choose because we can, or because we can't seem not to. Sometimes we quite simply want what we want like the children we once were. As adults, though, we should know better. Being one of God's own requires self-denial. Taking care of ourselves involves the same. Too much of the time, though, we stubbornly go our own way, exercising that free will to keep our human appetites sated.

It shows. The human right to choose and how we have implemented our will to fulfill those options has created a whole world of hurt. Wouldn't it just be simpler, and maybe even better, if the Lord made our choices for us?

If that were so, we'd all still be living in the Garden of Eden!

Quite simply, the Father needs to know his own. He will not force himself on us. He will not command our love. Instead our Father has set out clear standards showing how we are to find our way to him. How we choose to live up to them is on us. God's way requires that we get comfortable with obedience and denial of self. It's not an easy journey. The exercise of our free will in our choices over a lifetime will brand us as one of his. Or not.

It's a lesson that dates to his Garden.

INTERCESSION

Lord God, I can't blame my failures on anyone else. I know that deep down, but it's so easy to find reasons to explain away my bad choices. It's the same old story; even when my spirit is willing, my flesh is weak.

And my God spoke in answer to me thus: "It is not your will that fails you, my child. It is your desire. I gave you free will to protect you. It is the strongest of my gifts that come from the Spirit.

The problem is the desire for what is not for you. This world is not the paradise you were promised. This world is your crucifixion, not your reward. It is your journey and the place where you carry your cross. Jesus, my Son, faced choices as well. Why do you think he cried out to me in the Garden before they came for him? Asking me to take that bitter cup from him? He prayed for strength. When his humanity felt insufficient to the task, he did the next best thing, he gave his will to me. I remember the very words: "Father, not my will, but yours be done".

Perhaps you should do the same?

There is no place in your journey that you cannot ask me for strength. I have all you need. Turn to me in your need and I will support you with my almighty arm.

Be not of desire or of need. Be free of all with me."

As you say it, Lord. Amen.

> **John 15:4-5** *Abide in me and I in you. A branch cannot bear fruit unless it abides in the vine, neither can you unless you abide in me. I am the vine and you are the branches. Whoever abides in me and I in him bears much fruit- for apart from me you can do nothing.*

THE KILLING FIELD

He was the eldest son. That was one fortunate thing. It came with certain privileges. When his father passed, he would inherit the land. Along with the property, he would follow in his dad's footsteps as the village elder-in-charge. Then he would finally get the respect and authority he deserved! Surely, that day could not be too far off. In the meantime, he worked hard cultivating the fields.

His brother, Abel, tended the sheep. Their jobs were well suited, Cain thought. The brothers were very different from each other. Cain was strong and physically imposing. His work was demanding, and he put in long days. Abel, on the other hand, was a different sort; physically slight, quiet and gentle by nature. No doubt the long hours he spent in the hills watching over the flock were much occupied with deep contemplation and prayer.

Abel was generous, too, with what was theirs. Anyone who gave him a sad story could walk away with something to eat. He would pray with them, too, as though that would make everything all right.

His father, Adam, and Abel were like two peas in a pod, both made of the same devout and humble cloth. The whole village saw them as holy men. Cain, not so much. While he should have been the favorite son as heir, his father was not so pleased with him most of the time. His temper was easily provoked, and he could be physically combative. Even as a youngster, he was always testing the limits, challenging the doctrine and generally getting into trouble. Contrary to Cain's nature, Abel never questioned Adam's teachings or took issue with his viewpoint.

Cain could not make peace with their circumstances, either. He hated to see his parents prostrating themselves and groveling still for forgiveness over that long-ago transgression in the garden. When was atonement enough? To his way of thinking, if the heavenly Father of Eden was so great, then why did he even give his parents a choice in the first place? He could have controlled them by fear alone if he was so powerful a presence. His mother said their lives where hardscrabble now because of her own selfish disobedience when she was young.

Personally, Cain thought the two of them might have been set up. Any time you told someone not to do something, it was, in his experience, a certain draw to the opposite. At least for him. The whole thing ate at him. Because of his parents' trespass, he'd lost the chance to have an easy life in paradise—and he hadn't even been born yet! Why should he have to pay for the sins of his parents?

Today was a perfect example of his frustration. Every year each household offered a sampling of the best of their crops and animals to the Lord. His family presented a reaping of the field harvests and a fat yearling from their stock. The annual event never failed to set Cain off. It was such a waste, in his opinion. What sense did it make to give the best of their hard-won yield to appease a God who neither ate nor drank? How did the rest of them think they'd manage without his efforts in the fields? He was the one who put in the physical toil that ensured a good harvest.

That day, something inexplicable happened. Abel sacrificed their lamb, and all went as planned. Cain's crop offerings came next. He was stunned, along with everyone else in the community gathering, when they failed to catch fire on the sacrificial altar. They repeatedly tried to strike a flame with no result. The shock and consternation on his father's face and the sad disappointment in his mother's eyes made it clear that whatever the cause, Cain had failed to please the Lord. They were devastated and ashamed. They did not speak to Cain, but simply turned their backs and went home, his father shaking his head and muttering to himself. They were always like that: quick to judge and find fault with him. If that wasn't humiliation enough, Abel came over to him, urging him to humble himself and to think about how he had offended the Lord, assuring him there was mercy if he would simply embrace God's will. It was just too much. He angrily brushed Adam's hand off his shoulder and stalked into the hills.

Over the next few hours, Cain's rage did not subside. With the voice in his head urging him on, jealousy and a need for retaliation plagued his thoughts. The anger that emboldened him would not be denied and steadily whipped him into a frenzy of hate. He couldn't take any more, so he hatched a plan.

Walking back to the house that evening, he went to Abel and expressed his regrets, asking for his forgiveness. Abel, so grounded in the Lord's ways, of course responded with an embrace and a prayer that the Lord would guide him. *So typical*, thought Cain. He thought himself so superior, so much better.

Cain gritted his teeth in response and asked Abel if he would come over to the west field to take a look at his progress. He'd planned it well, and once Abel showed up, he slew him in a fury of vengeance. In shock, he remembered standing over Abel's inert body, blood pouring from the wound in his head. It had happened so fast. When he realized what he'd done, Cain panicked. Of course, the comforting voice in his head had no comment now. He ran into the hills and hid out the rest of the day. Later he denied any knowledge when asked where his brother was. When the truth came out, his mother wailed, and his father fell to his knees.

Punishment was swift. Cain was exiled to the land of Nod, east of Eden. He was never to return and his name never to be spoken again in his home village. He would never inherit. He would never have the respect he so coveted. His life as he knew it was over.

For the first time, though, Cain was finally first*: the first to kill.*

CONTEMPLATION

The Lord sees all. There are Christians who parrot the words and live the actions that speak of pious men. They do so with a purpose, and it does not have anything to do with their faith. Whatever discontent lies in their hearts, they hide it well from others, but they cannot disguise the truth from the Lord.

Perhaps Cain's sacrifice was not acceptable because his heart was not in it? He did what he had to do in view of his community and his goals for the future, but he was full of denial, resentment, and disbelief. God could not acknowledge such an imperfect offering. It would be false, and in the Lord, there is only truth.

With the hardships of the new world after Eden, Cain would not be alone in his trespasses for long. As the population grew, so sin ran amok for a long time after the Lost Garden. Like Cain, men and women were full of jealousy, pettiness, anger, and all manner of turmoil. The Old Testament shows the Father intervened many times, selecting and guiding individuals as prophets and leaders to his people. Even they struggled. The relationship between the Father and his children was weak after Eden. Something more would have to be done to heal that rift.

Moses was one of those chosen to show the way. Moses was called to the mountain and came back with the Ten Commandments.

If we look closely, the Lord based these laws on our own sure weaknesses; the very shortcomings Satan would exploit in the battle for our souls. The first choice for disobedience to God's command in Eden gave him that entrée. Eve disobeyed her Father, coveted what was not hers, stole from the Tree of Knowledge, made Adam complicit in her actions, and then lied about it. It was truly a train wreck of sins.

The insight the Father offers us is in the knowledge that no sin is singular. Most require or lead us into others. Satan doesn't need to settle for just one. He would encourage us to blame God for our troubles, to demean him and try to replace him with idols like money, prestige and power. Coveting others' possessions, acting with disobedience, lying, stealing, even killing to get what we want comes easily after.

It's as though the Father, knowing the challenges we would face, gave us rules of conduct that addressed every major portal to sin. In his love, even after we hurt him so badly, he tried to "even" up the ante. His Ten Commandments were to make us aware of our human weaknesses and how even one surrender can metamorphose into a calamity of others. Following his laws would protect us from those vulnerabilities; obedience to them would thwart the enemy.

We are so favored in the Father's love! His ancient gift of rules showed his people then and in our own time, how the battle for our souls would be fought. They made us aware of just where the enemy would strike so we were better prepared. Obedience to them is a certain map for victory!

All we need to do is submit, and that's the rub. *Obedience is not a strength that human beings embrace easily.* Adam and Eve were certainly not alone in that reality.

There is one commandment, the one to rest on the Sabbath, that might seem out of sync with the rest. Most of the rules are about what we cannot do; this one demands that we "do". While it may seem disconnected from the others, in truth, it's important to the rest in a unique way.

When we are at work without rest, we become vulnerable to unwise choices and decisions. To toil unceasingly is disrespectful of our health and the limits of our human bodies. It contributes to stress, disease, pain, and accidents. Most importantly, it shows disrespect to our Creator as the Being who fathered us. It also changes our focus from what is good for us and detracts from what should be motivating us.

Our spiritual health is of primary importance to the Father. When life gets too busy, we don't make time for spiritual renewal. We push too hard and then we tire and get cranky, intolerant, and irritable. We lose focus, take offense more easily, fly off the handle, react harshly, and in all of it, become prone to Satan's ever-vigilant influence.

That day of rest commandeered for the Lord is a day of needful healing for the body, mind, and spirit. It keeps us stronger against temptation. It pays homage to the Lord who created us. In our ignorance, we may not have chosen it for ourselves, so the Lord commanded we do it for him. He is truly deserving of our praise and worship. He is acting as our Protector. He knows there are serious consequences in not making time for precious communion with him and interaction with our committed church family. In those moments, we are strengthened.

What more could you ask for when your eternal life is at stake?

INTERCESSION

Lord, I never realized how one sin can follow another, and another. When I am tempted, I am focused on my desire, fighting to maintain my equilibrium, balancing what I want so badly against the reasons I must not be swayed. It doesn't occur to me committing one wrongdoing is rarely a singular trespass. How naïve I am!

It's a good thing my Father knows me better than I do! Long ago, he saw I would need a set of "rules" to combat my liabilities. He designed a personal battle plan that would lead me to victory. He based it on my own vulnerabilities as a human being!

When Adam and Eve opened that portal to the enemy in the garden, they opened a floodwall of desires and conflicting emotions that would forever create an ongoing skirmish for my soul. Even then, after so great a trespass, my Father did not forsake me, so great was his love for me. He knew that Satan would have an edge in the battle for my soul if he did not arm me well and prepare me for the unforeseen vagaries of war. He so wanted me to find my way back to him, he gave me the means to ensure my journey home in the form of Ten Commandments.

From that time forward, I need never be caught off guard. There would be no unexpected surprises in the enemy's camp.

Despite my many imperfections, and maybe in defense of them, the Father provided me with the map to Eternal Life by giving me a specific plan to follow.

What wondrous wisdom has the Lord shown! Praise his holy name in joy and thanksgiving.

> **Ephesians 6:10–18** *Finally be strong in the Lord and in the strength of his might. Put on the whole armor of God, that you may be able to stand against the schemes of the devil. For we do not wrestle against flesh and blood, but against the rulers, against the authorities, against the cosmic powers over this present darkness, against the spiritual forces of evil in the heavenly places. Therefore, take up the whole armor of God, that you may be able to withstand in the evil day, and having done all, to stand firm. Stand therefore, having fastened on the belt of truth, and having put on the breastplate of righteousness.*

THE HANDMAIDEN

She was just a girl. It was just an ordinary day. Then, not so much.

She remembered a blinding light. It appeared out of nowhere. She'd had to shield her eyes from the impact, falling helplessly to her knees.

At first, she was confused. Curiously, though, she was not afraid. Slowly, the light took on the most beautiful form. It literally took her breath away. A great peace fell upon her. Then a voice unlike any she had ever heard spoke these words:

"Hail Mary. Thou art full of grace. The Lord is with thee. I come from on high to bring you greetings in the Father's name and to speak the Lord's plan for you."

Mary sensed immediately that this moment would change her life. She couldn't help but wonder if she was dreaming. Why would the Almighty send a heavenly messenger to her, a young girl with but an ordinary life? Still, she responded, "I am truly the servant of the Lord. What is it the Father would ask of me?"

The Messenger replied, "You are to bear the Promised Savior of old, the Son of God who will bring the ancient prophesies to fruition."

Mary was well aware of the ancient prophesies. Her people had been waiting patiently for centuries and suffered much for their faith in the Lord's promise of redemption. What a blessing it would be if truly the time was at hand!

Timidly, Mary asked, "How can that be? I would serve as his handmaiden, but I know no man."

The heavenly visitor responded, "The Creator of all things, he who brought forth man from dust, knows no limits. He will fill you with his Holy Spirit and bring your womb to life. If you will trust in him, great things shall come to pass in you."

"As he wills it shall it be." replied Mary.

A short time later, Mary awoke as from a deep sleep. She recovered herself, unsure of how much time had passed. There was no light. There was no messenger. She was just as she'd been. Was it real? Who could she share it with? No one would believe her. Even her mother would be right to ask just how she found herself worthy to be the instrument of the Lord above all others.

Mary did not have answers. It occurred to her as well if all of this actually came to pass, she would find herself an outcast among her own. An unmarried woman with child would be disgraced. Her parents would be devastated. Her small devout community would be aghast. It became clear exactly what her agreement entailed. Yet she could never refuse her Lord. Perhaps she was simply mistaken.

After a couple of days of increasing concern, she decided to visit her favorite cousin Elizabeth in Judah to distract her mind from its persistent questing. Elizabeth was already with child. As Mary approached her, Elizabeth felt her womb leap for joy and the Spirit came upon her.

She spoke: "Blessed are you among women, and blessed is the fruit of your womb, Mary." Startled, Mary heard Elizabeth continue, "In you, fulfillment of all which has been spoken of for so long will come to pass."

With joy and gratitude, Mary realized that her loving Father had sent her the peace that comes with confirmation. Whatever the cost, he had honored her and would care for her. Her place in destiny would come to pass.

CONTEMPLATION

The Holy Book does not say much from here until the census that required Mary and her then husband, Joseph, to report to Bethlehem. Mary clearly was at term when they arrived.

How was Mary's news of her pregnancy received by her people? It isn't hard to imagine. The months she spent in her community undoubtedly were not pleasant. Many did not question her "visitor." They just didn't believe he was anything but a man. Would you?

Mary must have stubbornly refused to recant her story. A marriage was undoubtedly arranged for her with Joseph, an older and devout man who was willing to overlook the circumstances. Still, people being what they are, surely the reality did not merely go away.

Was it simply chance, then, that took Joseph and Mary from their immediate surroundings? Or did the Father have a hand in the census demand that required them to leave? Certainly, it was both a burden and a blessing. Traveling in her condition for that distance was not advisable, but failing to arrive in time for the census was even less so. Is anything in God's hands of random assignment?

Do you notice that in the Bible, God consistently asks impossible things of the people who are most faithful to him? Mary is a good example, but certainly not the only one, both in the Bible and in our own lives. She was the beginning of his plan to redeem mankind. Imagine if Mary had said, "No thank you Lord, I cannot bear the complications?"

Even so, he did not protect her from the certain costs that would come with the circumstances in her small, traditional Jewish community. Clearly, doing God's will does not guarantee an easy time of it. Rather, those who would honor the Father's callings find the prices in human terms often higher than they anticipated paying.

Our lives as Believers reflect the same contradictory truth. On how many occasions have we chastised our Lord when we are putting ourselves out on his behalf and difficulties continually bar our way? How many times have we seen others, so close to the Lord, seemingly so much more deserving of his blessings than we might perceive ourselves to be, pay more than their share in misery, death, or disaster?

If we are truly faithful to the Lord, we want to trust that our lives will be blessed by him, and that we will know his bounty in return. Today, there are even those who teach doing God's will assures us abundance here on earth. The truth is, we are seldom prepared for what comes on the heels of our commitment to the Almighty. If we turn to his Holy Book, that current belief is not as justified as we might think.

If Jesus himself was no exception as the very Son of God, does that not speak to us of a reality that is different? His great sacrifice did not net him what he surely deserved on this earth. His reward was death—a degrading, extremely painful, humiliating death. His reward came after.

Do not lose faith if all does not come to pass in your life as you would have it. Remain steadfast in the Lord, for we may put on the armor of Christ and pledge ourselves to his cause, but we still must be prepared.

The ravages of war are hardship and pain, even for those who are victorious in battle.

INTERCESSION

Heavenly Father, I know that you did not spare many of your faithful children from the harsh and painful realities that following your will created for them here on this earth. Your Book is full of stories about those who honored you above all and yet had to make terrible sacrifices. You asked Abraham, who you promised to raise up as the Father of all Nations, to sacrifice his son. You asked Mary, a young and pious girl, to have her reputation destroyed with her agreement to bear our Savior. You required your only Son to live a marginal life and to accept a painful and harrowing death. The Bible abounds with such tales.

The changes wrought upon the people we celebrate and admire in the Bible clearly speak to us. They are the ones we take as examples, the ones who stand firm in their faith even in the harsh glare of less palatable realities. They live in the eye of the storm.

As must we all.

> **Matthew 6:19–21** *"Do not store up for yourselves treasures on earth, where moths and vermin destroy, and where thieves break in and steal. But store up for yourselves treasures in heaven, where moths and vermin do not destroy, and where thieves do not break in and steal. For where your treasure is, there your heart will be also."*

JOSEPH THE FAITH-FULL

*E*veryone would take him for a fool.

How could he explain himself? If he said to them, "An angel told me it is so," what would they think? As he worked steadily at his trade, his thoughts continued independently of his labor, the wood taking form under his skillful hands.

For as long as he could remember, he'd been aware of Mary. He'd known her since she was a girl and he a youth. As a teenager, he'd teased her unmercifully. Then, as a young man, found himself trying to draw out her shy, reserved nature.

Their families were friends, and it was a small community of tradesmen, so there were occasions for the families to socialize. She was like a younger sister to him. Some time had gone by, though, before that day. When he thought back, that day changed everything. He smiled as he remembered.

Mary, a young woman now, had come to the market with her family. They'd all stopped at his father's business to catch up on one another's lives. He'd been busy setting out tools in the lean-to when he heard sweet, girlish laughter filtering back to the dimly lit shop. Curious, he leaned around the wood portal and saw her: Mary. She had truly grown into a beautiful woman. When she flashed him an impish smile and walked toward him, he felt flushed and suddenly awkward.

There was a light about her—a sense of joy that followed in her wake like a gently stirred wind chime on a spring day. She'd always had it, even as a child. Then one day she was suddenly a poised and spirited young lady, and clearly his feelings were no longer the feelings of a surrogate brother.

He wasn't the only one he was sure. Everyone knew Mary. He didn't know about the others, but, whenever he caught sight of her, something in his heart leapt within his chest. She was so good, so caring and compassionate, so pious in all her ways. A young, beautiful girl like that had her pick of partners.

It wasn't like he'd been without certain opportunities himself. His family let him know they were long out of patience with his disinterest in taking a wife. What was he saving his special self for, his mother would chide him? Yet he was content, and it seemed lately never more so than when Mary was nearby. Nothing could compare to the happiness she brought into his life.

But then, what chance had he? There were others of greater wealth and expectations than he -and certainly many younger. Yet, he stubbornly rationalized, there were other young women married to older men, and they were happy.

Mary understandably had offers for her hand. She treated them all with kindness and respect, but he'd also heard that she had shown her favor to no one. She would have to choose, soon. Why couldn't he speak his mind? It wasn't like him. Distracted, he laid aside his tools. How was he to end this misery, and why couldn't he untie his tongue around her?

One day a few weeks later, Mary came alone to the shop. She walked the short distance to where Joseph was working and paused. As he looked up, her eyes were warmly and steadily fastened on his own, a glint of teasing laughter sparking them with golden flecks like the sun. There was something about that look. It wasn't the same; there was an easy certainty, even a challenge in her manner.

"Why do you avoid me, Joseph?" she had teased gently. "I have missed you this month past."

That was the beginning. Good thing he'd had no premonition of what their love would bring upon them, or God's plans for them!

Later, when she told him she was with child, he was stunned. When she further informed him an angel told her she was carrying the promised Savior and she had lain with no man, he didn't know what to think. She couldn't be in her right mind. When he thought of the repercussions, he ached for her. His heart was broken. He didn't know what to say, so staggered was he with the shock of it. He could not speak a word, but his struggle must have been plain on his face. Mary had fled without another word, silent tears running down her face. How devastating it must have been for her. What could she expect? What was he to do? How could he protect her? He was frantic with fear and almost prostrate with grief, torn for her pain and for his own.

That night, he'd had a visitor. He wasn't dreaming. The message was clear. It brought him joy and relief and awe. He couldn't believe it at first, but he knew in his heart it was not his imagination. He loved Mary, and she was to be his. The Messenger had told him so.

Let others say what they would. Joseph was not one for understanding things that made no sense, but he was one for knowing God's ways were not ways a man questioned lightly. It was his destiny, and he would stand by Mary.

Was he up to the task? He didn't know. He had his doubts—but he knew one thing for sure: God was.

CONTEMPLATION

We've all been fools for love. The experience changes us. Whether we are beginners in love or old-timers who know its ways, we can probably agree on one thing: love is a journey fraught with peril. There is no other feeling like it. The emotions can take us to the highest of summits or plunge us into the deepest ravines of despair. The strongest among us can find ourselves meek as lambs. It can confuse the most secure, causing us to question our own good sense.

When love doesn't work out to our expectations, there are other kinds of changes. Some of us become determined never to be compromised again. Others armor themselves, protecting the vulnerability that caused their pain. They don't trust their feelings and become guarded in their emotions. More than a few find it easier to just take themselves out of the game altogether.

Surely Joseph was susceptible to all these emotions. Every feeling must have passed through him at being told the love of his life was with child. He could, without cen-sure, have taken any one of the paths open to him. He could have despaired of love altogether, become enraged with the unfairness of it all, passed ruthless judgement and lived on as a closed and bitter man. He could have cursed God and defied his lack of intervention. Joseph knew full well what he would suffer at the hands of the strict community if he chose to believe, accept, and give his love to Mary.

However, Joseph was a Believer. He also knew that while God offers each of us his love freely, it doesn't come without a commitment to his ways. Often, those ways are not easy.

He knew others would not understand. He knew that God was not going to help them in their ignorance. Yet the Holy Visitor's message was stunningly clear in its simplicity: the time of the Promised Savior was at hand!

Joseph knew better than to ask for answers. He knew true faith requires that we act *before* we have all the answers.

INTERCESSION

Holy Father, when did I become intent on knowing it all? When did I come to believe that by applying my own very limited human resources, I might come to know your infinite mind and your vision for my Universe?

My years here on this earth are few and will pass quickly. I am surely but a blink of your almighty eye in that eternal vista. Yet, you have a plan for me. You have a love for me.

I am unworthy and weak, Lord, and prone to failing us both. I want to control my destiny. I can't seem to let go of being in charge. Joseph could have refused you; he had free will. He couldn't have known he would change history with his answer. As for the rest of the world and how they would feel, Joseph knew, as I would do well to remember, that the salvation of my soul is not in the judgment of the majority around me, but in the singular measure of the Father's love for me.

May I find a little Joseph in me, Lord.

> **Proverbs 3:5–6** *Trust in Jehovah with all your heart and do not lean upon your own understanding. In all your ways take notice of him, and he himself will make your paths straight.*

THE HAPLESS INNKEEPER

It wasn't his fault.

Business hadn't been this good in years. In fact, wasn't it just last month he had seriously considered packing up his family and moving to Jerusalem to try his hand at something more lucrative? Now that blessed edict demanding all subjects return to their original villages for counting had granted him a reprieve. The money he earned from all those weary travelers passing through or arriving in Bethlehem would carry him for a very long time.

He looked again. Surely, he felt sorry for them; she heavy with child, he obviously travel-weary and filled with misgivings. They were but two of hundreds. What could he do? He had no room at the inn. Every square inch of space was occupied. Every inn in town was the same.

He had no time, either, to brood over a common laborer and his wife. Babies were born every day. They'd manage. In the meantime, his clientele clamored for more bread and mead, and they paid in good coin. Opportunity did not loiter. Best send them on their way and get back to the business at hand—that was the plan.

He paused. The stable. A small cave out of the wind and weather where the animals were bedded for the night. They could have the stable. What was it about this pair? Well, it didn't matter. The sooner he saw them settled, the sooner he could get back to work. He looked them over carefully once more. Would they take offence? It wasn't much, and they'd have to share it with the stock. It was clean, though—he'd seen to it himself earlier that day.

He shrugged his shoulders. They could take it or leave it. He wasn't going to waste another minute feeling sorry for a couple who hadn't the good sense to prepare ahead for the inevitable. It wasn't that he was without compassion. He was as good as the next man—better than most. With a sigh, he led them out the front door of the inn and pointed in the direction of what shelter he had to offer.

Now, for his generosity, everybody knew him not by his name, but by his occupation. Most of all for his nefarious deed: he was the foolish innkeeper who turned away the Son of God, causing him to be born in a lowly manger.

What more could he have done?

CONTEMPLATION

Most of us can relate to the poor innkeeper. He did not know the future. He was very much in the present and feeling grateful for circumstances that gave him reason to hope for some better times ahead.

God tells us we are all innkeepers. The hungry, the homeless, the needy, the unloved and the outcasts of our society are knocking on our doors. Like the innkeeper, we get busy in our day-to-day lives; we are preoccupied with taking care of us and ours. We can't be concerned with providing for anyone else. There are only so many hours in a day, and there seem to be so many of them, always in need.

We reason, let them go to work. Better they had planned or prepared ahead or tried harder. Maybe they should have considered today when they dropped out, picked up that bottle, lit up that first joint, took that first hit, or got lazy. After all, we had the same choices. We did the right thing. How are we responsible for them? We are impatient, even angry with their unrelenting insistence. We don't have time. We don't have room. We don't want to get involved. We certainly don't want to encourage their expectations. Why don't they find a job, go home to their families, get some training? You know, lift themselves up by their own bootstraps? Maybe start with a bath and a haircut?

Besides, you help one, and a dozen more spring up to take their place. You know that whatever you give them will be wasted on drugs or drink anyway. Why encourage them?

Surely, our arrogance knows no bounds. But for the grace of God go any one of us. There are no guarantees in life, and not many of us that haven't pushed the limits of reasonable behavior at some point—pushing limits that might have claimed us as well as that person on the street. *Going without is not synonymous with being a loser.* Even if it was, who are we to sit in judgment of anyone?

It's not that we're unfeeling, Lord. We do what we can. *What more do you want?*

INTERCESSION

Lord, open my eyes to the ways of Christ, your Son. Remind me that it was not his way to coddle himself with the approval of those around him who were well off. He lived by his own choosing among the poor, the lepers and the ill. He walked among them and ate with them and slept in their poor dirt-floored homes. When they were hungry, he did not look to someone else to provide. He fed them loaves and fishes until they had their fill. He did not deprive those he surely knew to be undeserving. He did not judge who should have and who should not. Nor did he wind his way around the physically repulsive and the beggars, instead embracing them in his healing ways. The grotesque and the damaged did not repel him. He did not send a disciple to touch them or to deliver his life-saving healing for him.

He was out among the crowds, aware, working all the time and meeting people where they lived. He understood their human needs were great. He knew he brought them even more than they sought: the sustenance of God's love that their Spirits would never go hungry. He gave them acceptance without judgment and love without rancor. For many, he gave hope where there had once been only despair.

Jesus did more than simply give us a blueprint, Father. He made it amply clear that we cannot distance ourselves from those who are in need and call ourselves one with him. *He would teach us that the gift just past willing compliance is by far the greater gift.*

I would learn that lesson, Lord, and live my life accordingly.

John 1:41 *But if someone who is supposed to be a Christian has money enough to live well and sees a brother in need and won't help him—how can God's love be within him?*

THE FAVORED ONE

He didn't get it.

He was supposed to be the good guy. Hadn't he stayed here and worked his tail off these past few years? Hadn't he listened to the old man ceaselessly lament the loss of his younger son and wail long and wearily about his fate? He'd gritted his teeth and bit back his retorts time after time, resolutely keeping his opinions to himself and spending his exasperation on hard work instead. It was his blood, sweat, and tears that had made the farm what it was today. It was a near thing, though, after his father had given his brother half of the inheritance that belonged to him as the eldest. Only his own perseverance and dogged determination over the years had gradually paid off.

As time went on with no word from his brother, the resentment gradually lessened. He did wonder occasionally what had befallen his errant sibling. Had he realized his illusive fortune? He didn't really know how he felt about that. It wasn't like he wanted him to fail, exactly. Then again, there were other times he felt that losing it all was exactly what he deserved. His brother had always been a dreamer, looking for the easy way out. Even so, he'd never in his wildest imagination pictured this scenario: the long-lost rebel suddenly resurrected on this very spot.

You'd think he'd be too ashamed to return home—with all that money gone, too. Reduced to working with swine the worst of it. It was against all they believed in. The whole family would be shamed. Yet the Old Man was killing the best yearling and pulling out all the stops for a feast? Had he lost all sense? And when was the last time he himself even had an appreciative comment from his dad?

He threw down his shovel in disgust.

He heard his father come up behind him.

"Daniel," he said, "I know that your heart is troubled with resentment and anger towards your brother, who has at long last come back to us."

"Son, don't you know that I have always loved you? Cannot you rejoice with me that one who was lost to us has returned to the family fold? We'd be happy if one of our own lost lambs were recovered unhurt, how much more should our welcome be for one of our own?"

Maybe. It was good to see the old man light up with joy, the strain and worry of years sliding away from his furrowed brow. Rachel, his wife, had tried to tell him often enough: love was the one commodity—maybe the only one—that truly never ran short.

Life. Go figure. With a shrug of his shoulders and a last exasperated glance heavenward, he turned to walk his dad back and to join in his family's good fortune. *He might have to accept it, but he didn't have to understand it.*

CONTEMPLATION

How many times, Lord, has a family member left me feeling angry, resentful, and apart? How many times have I seethed with hostility at a promotion that went to someone else, or at a friend's trespass I can't let go? What about those people with charmed lives—the ones who seem to always land on their feet, or those who prosper at the ruin of others? What about the shirkers, the braggarts, the complainers, the screw-ups, and the ungrateful I run into every day? Those family members who have more, or who get more, or who surely are loved more; being the favorites? What about the arrogance and the idleness of all those self-absorbed people that expect me to cater to their expectations? What has your love got to do with it?

Don't you know you're asking the impossible, Lord? Others have strayed long and hard from your designated path, while I have walked with forbearance and commitment. I have sacrificed and labored ceaselessly according to your laws, yet it seems that all around me, others are reaping undeserved rewards. As for those who have caused me such personal pain, you clearly expect me to welcome them back into my heart.

It's a frustration, Father. It seems there are always people around us who aren't toiling in your fields. Instead, they've been busy indulging themselves for years while we may have felt the urge but resisted the temptation. Then, there are neighbors, co-workers, families, bosses, friends, children, partners—all of them can and do let us down.

Your way is a little much, Lord. I mean, I get it. In my head, I can see your reasoning. But real life, Lord—that is something else. *Forgiveness is hard enough, and it's harder still when no one even asks for it.* To give it anyway, and without resentment or judgment, is asking a lot.

But Lord, here's the thing - you don't stop there, though, do you?

I have to be *happy* about it!

INTERCESSION

I'm going to need a lot of help here, Lord. Your path isn't an easy one. Letting go of the grievances, the slow burning resentments, the petty judgments, the old grudges isn't going to be painless. Some of them are well and truly deserved. Why should I be the one to relent and humble myself? You expect me to welcome those losers and traitors back into my life, to forgive their very real and personal trespasses and more than that, to do so in celebration of their return?!

What's that, Lord?

Well, yes, I guess if anyone could stand on righteousness, it's you, Lord.

What's that you say, Lord?

Riotous giving? Unlimited forgiving?

Lord help me.

Lord help us all. Please.

Ephesians 4:31–32 *Let all bitterness and wrath and anger and clamor and slander be put away from you, along with all malice. Be kind to one another, tender-hearted, forgiving one another, as God in Christ forgave you.*

MARY THE STONED

From the time she was a little girl, she'd had to scratch in the dirt for enough just to get by. Hunger and cold had been her constant companions; love a stranger to her. Her mother had died giving birth. Her father found her of no account. Drunk much of the time, she was left to fend for herself. The day came when he grew tired of her favors and sold her off to a traveling vender. She went from one horrible situation to another. Eventually she ran away.

That was the beginning of life on her own. Nothing of any value belonged to her. Times were desperate, and her beauty was all she had. It only made sense that it was hers to use. It alone brought her any kindness, fleeting though it may be.

At first, it was a blessing. There was food to eat and a warm place to sleep. She had friends and nice clothes. Sometimes, if she closed her eyes, she could even imagine she belonged to one of her patrons. In the morning, though, it was always the same. She was alone.

Lately, she had grown tired and disillusioned. It was not so easy to see how much better her life was now. What good is food to one who has no appetite or warmth that flees in the cold light of day? Maybe she'd grown careless on purpose. Maybe she just didn't care anymore.

Where would the first stone find its mark? She cowered in the sand. There was no escape. Her degradation was exposed to all, weighing her down like the choices in her life until she had no strength to protest. The merciless heat of the sun beat down on her shamefully uncovered hair. Derisive shouts and name-calling came from all around her. People were kicking dirt in her face, spitting at her. There was nothing she could do.

Numbly, she thought about the unfairness of it all. Surely the wrath of any god who could condone such suffering could be no worse than the crowd who sought her life so cruelly this day? Hypocrites, all of them. At least she had an excuse. She was a born loser. Her father had told her so often enough. What did it matter now? Soon it would all be over. Closing her eyes, she steeled herself for the pain.

Suddenly a hush fell over the crowd. She heard the voice, the voice of her angel, calling her name. Then he spoke to the crowd,

"Let him who is without sin cast the first stone."

The ensuing silence hurt her very ears. All was still for a moment, and then the muttering began. She heard the dull thumps of stones hitting the ground. She sensed people moving away from her. She held her breath. Dare she look? Slowly, she raised her head. Only a few curious onlookers remained. Then she saw him.

He was writing in the dirt, and the message was a revelation to her. He extended his hand. Helping her to rise, he spoke with gentleness and love. "My daughter, go and sin no more."

It was a command for then, and for now.

CONTEMPLATION

We are all victims of where we come from. We are victims by nature of where we are born into our families: eldest, youngest, middle child. We are raised by parents who are products of their parents. As life goes on, events outside our control can victimize us as well. People can make choices without our best interests in mind and change our lives in ways we don't want. Others' actions, prejudices, and secrets can affect us even as we are ignorant of them. Being victimized does not require our consent, or even our cooperation. Mary's situation is a perfect example of this. Sometimes the impact of others on our lives makes it nearly impossible to turn things around.

Mary felt the desperation of being helpless to change her circumstances. Mary did not know Jesus. Without him, she could not know that we all have the ability and the challenge to choose differently—to turn victimization into victory. Jesus defeated even death. In him, all things are surmountable.

While life can make us feel like born losers, there is really no such thing. We are creatures of God, and as such, we are already winners. In the beginning, we come to this earth as pure potential. That clean slate has no preconceived notions and makes no judgements. We thrive on the love of our surrogate parents, who stand in for God's love here on earth. It is the one thing that makes us truly whole. It is also our one vulnerability. A child depends on a loving parent.

The devastating consequences of children being abandoned, beaten, abused, mistreated, neglected in infancy and young childhood is unfortunately all around us. The cost is a total perversion of what being human is about. This travesty breeds a lack of respect for life in general, a belief that taking is the only way to meet your needs, a belief that you are a mistake, that you are unlovable, that you have only yourself to depend on or to care about. The path it sets is not one of God's love for his children,

These parenting and environmental issues can play a devastating part in our development and how we view the world around us as grown adults. When we suffer as children, we can become compromised adults with low self-esteem and feelings of abandonment. It isn't easy, in that frame of mind, to believe that a heavenly Father has us in his heart and cares about what happens to us. To accept that long before we came to be in this world, we were in God's mind is not a lot of comfort. It's easy to suggest to the Father that if he anticipated our life, he was guilty for not changing it in the first place! Discussions of free will and human choices as the catalysts for the circumstances we're in are not so well received either. *Without the knowledge of Christ's life and death, there is little courage born of misery.*

What the Father does offer to those who will open themselves to his word is more priceless than understanding: *it is hope.* Where our human family can fail us, the Father assures us he will not. He is compassionate and wise with an unending supply of the love we crave. *The dilemma is that someone must show us—someone who already knows.* As Believers, each of us could and should be that catalyst.

Jesus saw the emptiness and despair in Mary's heart. He touched her with love and acceptance, possibly for the first time in her life. The soul-hunger in her responded like a starving adult in the presence of a sumptuous banquet. No one had to explain. Her soul recognized the real thing and knew it for what it was.

Most importantly, Jesus placed a high value on her in those moments with the crowd. In front of all, he challenged the surly, bloodthirsty mob on their judgment of a common prostitute. He raised her up by doing so. He brought her and her judges to one level with a few simple words: "Let he who has no sin cast the first stone."

Mary was no longer a victim, but a human being, equal to all others. What wonder must have assailed her in that moment!

Was the message written in the sand about forgiveness? Perhaps with Jesus' forgiveness, Mary could finally forgive herself?

It changed her life.

Forgiveness changes all.

INTERCESSION

Let us pray, Lord, that we never despair. If you could defeat even death because of your unconditional love for us, we are indeed of worth to you and, in turn, to the world you have provided us.

Around us, so many are in need. It's easy to pass judgement, especially on the defensive, hostile, and belligerent people who spurn our concerns. That happens to a person when they see no way out. You would remind us that if we knew the circumstances of their life path, we might have more compassion and understanding.

While most of us struggle to overcome circumstances that seem unfair to us or that are holding us back, Mary's story shows that not everyone feels they have a chance to be different. Mary would have died except for Jesus' intervention. He set this example for a reason: to show it is up to us as blessed Believers to share the Good News with those who are ignorant of it and to offer the hope of finding a new path in Christ. If we do not, how will it come about?

Lord, in your eternal wisdom, show me how to be a shining example of your love and an active participant in spreading it to all who come into my life. Through your message of forgiveness and acceptance may I be a catalyst for hope in the lives of those paralyzed by unfairness and despair.

This is the command you have laid upon my shoulders: that all may be saved in the knowledge of Christ. Amen.

> *Isaiah 61: The Spirit of the Lord God is upon me; because the LORD anointed me to preach good tidings unto the meek; he hath sent me to bind up the brokenhearted, to proclaim liberty to the captives, and the opening of the prison to them that are bound;*

THE TREE HUGGER

He was doing it again. Talking to himself.

Guess it was becoming a habit. He didn't find conversation with others easily come by. Unworthy of the elite citizenry and detested by the commoners, you got used to being a loner in his line of work. Waiting patiently, he was perched precariously on the upper branches of an oak tree just east of the morning market. This gave him a good view of the boulevard all the way from the gates of the city. If all went well, he would not be easily observed.

While he waited, he thought about his work. No getting around it: he was a tax collector. There it was. Somebody had to do it. Besides, it was sort of a family tradition—probably because once your family got into that line of work, it wasn't so easy to get out. The truth was he probably couldn't get another job anyway, even if sometimes he wanted one. Everyone knew him. His family name was well known.

People all around guarded their tongues in his presence. He knew many cursed the Prelate's tax laws even if they risked charges of treason in doing so. Wouldn't they be surprised to find out his feelings weren't so far removed from theirs? Even if he agreed with them, he still had to collect it, and that made him a convenient target for all the rage and desperation around him. He was the one they hated to see walking down the street. While he'd really tried to develop a tough skin, like others in his line of work, it just wasn't in him.

He did his best providing for his own. The material rewards of the position made it easier to rationalize his unease. Some days it left a bad taste in his mouth, but he swallowed hard and went about his business. The isolation was too much, though. He might as well join the leper colony east of town.

It's just that he really wasn't a bad person. After all, he had to pay his taxes, too. It wasn't that he was without feelings, either. He wasn't like some; he never did take pleasure in his neighbors' hardships or take advantage of his professional standing.

Thing was, it never used to bother him this much. But times were hard and getting harder. He himself sold off some stock to make his share this year. He wouldn't barter his meagre self-respect with the chief treasurer for a reduction in his own take. He didn't want to "owe" that one any favors. Sometimes he wondered why - it's not like anyone else would believe that he didn't bribe his own way out of his dues anyway. It was a common enough practice.

The noise of the crowd drew him from his thoughts. A motley procession was moving slowly down the dusty street. They crowded in on Jesus from all sides. You really couldn't even see him yet, but only Jesus could attract a crowd like that one. Ever since he'd caught Mathias' eye last month on his way to the central office, he'd been uneasy. Those eyes; stopped him in his tracks they did. Sort of looked through you: riveting, captivating, unsettling all at one and the same time.

He'd made discreet inquiries into this Jesus of Nazareth. Interesting man. Foolish man. Probably not a man to associate with, the times being what they were. Still, the Messiah?

Mathias had tried to forget. Getting mixed up with the Nazarene would only make his job much harder—if he didn't lose it altogether. Still, this fascination wouldn't leave him in peace. He had to get one more look. At least disguised by the leaves, his plan was that his foolish curiosity would go unnoticed.

The crowd stopped just short of his perch. Jesus looked up at him. He could have been expecting him for all his surprise.

"Mathias," he spoke, "I am weary and hungry and look forward to the hospitality of your table tonight."

Had Mathias heard the words correctly? He almost fell out of the tree!

Surely the man knew *who* he was talking to? He looked around. Not many people populating trees these days. Jesus was talking to him, all right. The crowd quieted. Jesus waited patiently for an answer. Was that a twinkle in his eye?

Mathias' heart sang as he shouted, "Yes, Lord, I will make straight away to see to your comfort." He couldn't help himself.

As he raced off on joyous feet, he thought again that maybe he was in the wrong line of work. Could be it was time for a change. If Jesus gave him a chance, then surely others would too. You know, it felt pretty good to be a person again.

It beat hugging trees.

INTERCESSION

Many of us are tree huggers. We like to go unnoticed for all our piety. We don't want to be judged by those around us who might think our point of view foolish. Then again, we don't believe that God could love such a one as us anyway. We think about the deeds we've done, the secrets we carry, the damage we've caused. We rationalize our work, our home life, and our choices or lack of them.

We have enemies, and we've earned them. We aren't even people pleasers when you get right down to it. We might even be a bully. For sure, lots of us like to blend in. It's uncomfortable—if not downright dangerous—to stand out in our times.

We must admit, though, we are curious. His followers say Jesus accepts us all, loves us all—sinners and saints. Of course, what fools we'd be to believe that. Yet, what a wondrous relief to be accepted for who we are; to be known and yet free, frail and yet loved, flawed but not judged!

Had Jesus not called to Mathias that day, undoubtedly, he would have hugged that tree for dear life until the opportunity to know more had passed him by—out of fear and shame. But Jesus knew him. He knew his innermost heart and his conflicted state of mind. He saw fertile ground and a harvest for his Father. Jesus called to Mathias because to call was his anointed command. Once he called, he waited, patiently, for the return acknowledgement.

How embarrassing it must have been for Mathias to be exposed in all his vulnerability in front of the crowd! Jesus knew the thoughts that confused his mind and the desperate self-loathing he nursed deep in his heart.

Even so, he did take himself in hand. He did not make the Lord wait too long. He gave his answer and felt the joy of being loved and accepted.

Don't you wonder how long Jesus would have been prepared to wait for Mathias' reply? Can you see the crowd, suspended in time around the Man of Nazareth while he conversed and waited on the reply of the despised community Tax Collector? And then announced he was going to sup with him?

Like Mathias, hiding our true selves easily becomes a habit. We assume our outward identities defined by what we do, who we are called, who we associate with. Our world is full of all kinds of fig leaves that we can use to camouflage our real selves or to hide our genuine natures. There are as many of them as there are secrets we feel the need to protect others from knowing.

Are you avoiding Jesus? Keeping out of his way? Do you rationalize your life, your lack of commitment, and the circumstances that make it easy for you to live in your deliberate, comfortable nest of denial? Are you sitting in a tree of fear and selfishness, waiting for the branch to fall to save you from the choice?

Jesus requires you to make the decision. He wants you to answer his call, to acknowledge his love freely—*to choose him.*

INTERCESSION

Who am I kidding, Lord? I am so like Mathias. So insecure. So sensitive to how others see me. So vulnerable to their slights and judgments.

In my own defense, I am certainly not alone in these feelings, Lord. It's so awkward when I "stand out." I don't like facing derision or outright rejection by my peers. I just want to get along. Most of the time, that means not calling attention to myself, keeping up appearances like everyone else, learning the boundaries.

Yet you've made it clear, Lord, that you require more of me. You expect me to put your will ahead of my comfort. My very soul is at risk when I refuse to leave my "safe" place. When I stand in my faith as you've directed, I am not one of the crowd anymore. I am one of yours.

I pray Father that your Holy Spirit takes up residence in my heart as he did when your son's disciples cowered in fear after the death of Jesus. Your Holy Spirit came to them and filled them with courage, suffusing them with their calling. They were able to leave their panic room and go forth. Give me the same Lord, and I will proclaim your salvation to the world.

> **Jeremiah 23:23-24** *Can anyone hide himself in secret places that I shall not see him saith the Lord? Do not I fill heaven and earth saith the Lord?*

PETER THE ROCKED

He had set him apart.

This Man of Galilee he had come to love had pulled him from the sea as easily as once he himself had pulled his fishing nets to shore. Like the fish caught in his wake, he was helpless in the hands of this "Fisher of Men" as they—so strongly was he caught up in the Master's ways. He wasn't alone. There were eleven more just like him, all of them meekly ensnared in the same net and devoid of any desire to go back to their old ways.

Taking him aside that fateful night, Jesus singled him out of the twelve and bade him walk some little ways apart. Before he knew what had happened, Jesus sat him on a rock and placed the mantle of his calling securely on Peter's shoulders. He, Peter, didn't ask for that. It was too great a weight to carry—too much for a mere mortal man. Jesus then told Peter he would be leaving soon, and that Peter was to assume the leadership of his new following when he went to his Father. The Master had spoken of this leaving often, but Peter and the others did not understand, did not want to believe. Now he was saying the time was upon them? How was Peter to handle that?

He found himself sorely disturbed. Could he do such a thing? Would his friends and fellow disciples accept this new role? Things were getting increasingly dicey. Would anyone live long enough to go on? He looked around at the group gathered about the fire. They would expect—what? Miracles, no doubt. Already the others looked to him for answers he couldn't provide. He had none. He was a simple man, a fisherman by trade. His had been a hard life, but one that demanded no more than the sun and the sea required of him. How could the Lord expect this of him? He was no Jesus, that was for sure.

CONTEMPLATION

The disciples had been in Jesus' care from the beginning. They had left the only lives they'd known, unsure of how they and their families would even survive. Jesus became their security. He was their leader, their holy man, their teacher. They had willingly placed themselves in his capable hands.

Now, Jesus had placed them all in Peters'. This left Peter with a garden variety problem—the buck stopped with him. This was not so comfortable a place as being a right-hand man. Peter had his doubts. He was not ready, maybe even a little angry about this unexpected and unwelcome turn of events. Then Jesus told him he was leaving. Talk about going from the frying pan into the fire! The timing for being unavailable to his followers could not have been worse.

Peter no doubt had been perplexed and concerned about Jesus more than once. He didn't understand everything the Master said, but then Jesus had assured them all that in time, as they were ready, the understanding would come. How were they to learn if he was gone? Why must Jesus abandon his work and go home to his Father? What had it all been for?

The gospel doesn't tell us just how the rest of the twelve took this singling out. It's likely there was discussion about it, suspicion, maybe even jealousy and denial. That's what humans do when someone gets put in authority over them— particularly someone who was once of equal status. While his mentor was with him, Peter did not feel the full weight of leadership. Jesus was his cloak of security. Now so much had happened in such a short time. It was surely chaos with more to come.

After Jesus died, all the disciples fled in fear for their own lives. Peter followed Jesus. Already he had unknowingly assumed the mantel of leadership. His actions were directed by a need to know and in knowing, to figure out how to act. His concern was not just for himself and his mentor, but for all the Lord's disciples.

While Peter was not yet tested, not yet experienced in what it took to be a leader, Jesus knew that true leadership begins with knowing we are always a step from failing. He told Peter so when he said, "Before the cock crows the third time, you will have denied me thrice."

Peter would learn that a leader in Christ is forged in the fire, washed in humility, and baptized in faith. Reluctance has nothing to do with it.

INTERCESSION

Let us pray for discernment, Lord. In every capacity, aid us to choose leadership wisely. Enable us to see through to the man despite all the rhetoric and political maneuvering that surrounds him.

This world needs strong leaders who believe in God's ways. They are harder to find and increasingly difficult to recognize. Our times are ripe with disorder, chaos, and persecution because of it. We are paying with famine, disease, death, ethnic cleansing, and human misery.

Our world stage is being overrun by abuses of power. The suffering of so many is multiplying every day as leaders are seduced by greed and a megalomania that blinds them to God's will. We watch in horror, knowing that the Bible speaks of it all coming to pass. We feel overwhelmed and unprepared to stem the tide.

As God's chosen, we do not have the luxury of not getting involved. We need to recognize our apathy and feelings of helplessness are but tools in Satan's ongoing crusade. Just like he did with Peter the Lord has commanded us to take on the mantle of leadership in his name, and we are feeling the same lack of qualifications as Peter did.

The Father has faith in us. He has bestowed the calling of true Christian example on each of us. The actions of every Believer in these troubled times must be directed toward the return of God's kingdom on this earth and the promise of a peace that will endure for all time.

Timothy 4:2–5 Preach the word; be ready in season and out of season, reprove, rebuke and exhort, with complete patience and teaching. For the time is coming when people will not endure sound teaching but having itching ears they will accumulate for themselves teaches to suit their own passions and will turn away from listening to the truth and wonder off into myths. As for you, always be sober-minded, endure suffering, do the work of an evangelist, fulfill your ministry.

MUTINY AT GETHSEMANE

ight of them sat around the garden that night. Each one contemplating his own thoughts, nervously aware of the strange ambience that surrounded them. Conversation had been sporadic at best, and an uneasy silence held sway between them now. A shared sense of foreboding had taken hold as the hours of the night passed. Oddly subdued, they had gathered around the fire, uneasy with the flickering of light and shadow. It was as if ghosts walked the valley tonight, restless but invisible. They had not seen this side of the Master before, either. It didn't help. Something was in the wind.

At his request, they'd all come to pray with him at Gethsemane. Only Judas was inexplicably absent. When they arrived, Jesus had removed himself a little distance away, taking only Peter and the two Zebedee brothers with him. For some time now, they had been reluctant witnesses to the anguished and muffled pleas to his Father. It was clear that Jesus was not himself. All of them were troubled and exhausted with worry over his unsettling behavior. Emotionally drained, many had fallen asleep in the early morning hours.

Suddenly, Jesus came forward among them, upbraiding them and bidding them again to keep watch. *For what?* they wondered. *Is he losing his mind?*

Peter sought to comfort Jesus. He could see that he was deeply disturbed and preoccupied. In an attempt to ease his Master's concerns, he assured Jesus that his loyalty was unassailable and that he would be there at his side, whatever happened. He was stunned when Jesus said that awful thing; that Peter would deny him three times even before this night had passed. Protesting and hurt, Peter assured him on pain of death that it would never be so. He vowed to stay awake and protect his Lord throughout the night.

While he spoke, Peter heard a loud commotion, and Judas Iscariot, one of their own, suddenly came forward out of the shadows. He was not alone. There were armed guards with him. The disciples watched, stunned with events as they unfolded. Judas walked up boldly to Jesus and kissed him on the cheek.

It appeared to be a signal because the Centurion at Judas' side immediately grabbed Jesus. That action brought the disciples out of their inertia. Mark drew his sword in defense of his Master, slicing off the ear of the nearest soldier. While confusion and uncertainty reigned, Jesus remained unnervingly calm. Peter heard in disbelief as he chided Mark for his action and then calmly put the severed ear back in place, healing the wound and ordering them all to sheath their weapons. With that, the eleven were frozen with shock and confounded with fear. There was no sense to what was going on. They did as Jesus asked, but looked nervously at one another as he was led meekly away.

Peter decided to follow. He shadowed the armed guards furtively, hiding his face, anxious to see where they were taking Jesus. When they entered a building in the city proper, Peter huddled in the shadows of a nearby courtyard.

"Hey, there. You. Surely, you are one of the twelve?" an old man peered at him curiously.

"Are you blind, old man?" replied Peter.

The sound of a cock crowed in the distance.

Peter moved away. If he were to acknowledge his identity, they would take him as well. He placed his hands over a public brazier. He was just here to get some news about what was going on. He didn't dare show too much interest. He'd just rely on the bits and pieces he picked up while he blended in, unnoticed. Part of him was angry that his Master would bring them all to this. Part of him was fearful for his own life and for the others.

"Haven't I seen you with the Nazarene? Are you here with him now?" a young servant girl with a water jug inquired of him.

Peter replied testily, "Leave me be! Can a man have no peace? I am not one of them!" A cock crowed in the distance.

Peter was growing increasingly nervous. It seemed that everyone around him was looking at him with suspicion and curiosity. He didn't dare stay here much longer; they might decide to act on their own. He scuttled down a dark alley to the right. Someone coming out the other end bumped into his shoulder in passing.

"Aren't you the fisherman I've seen with that traitor Jesus? Surely I've seen your face in his company?"

"No, for the last time, I am not him," Peter snarled. "Would I be risking my life and limb hanging around here if I was?"

It was enough. Peter left, unnerved and afraid.

And then he heard the cock crow, again—and he remembered.

He hung his head in shame and misery.

CONTEMPLATION

Peter was not a coward. He loved his Lord. He was vehement in his insistence that nothing could tear him from Jesus' side. No doubt it shook Peter to his core to see this Man of God whom he had seen do so many impossible things suddenly in the hands of the enemy, and without protest.

Peter was not unlike any one of us when someone we admire and rely on suddenly falls from grace or fails to live up to our expectations. We become angry, distrustful, afraid and foolish by degrees. When our faith is tested, when our very church leaders fail us, we are left with an impossible question: if those we love and believe in turn out to be vulnerable to sin, where does that leave the rest of us? How can we trust our own judgement?

When we read the Bible about the end times to come, we are often caught up in the same "Peter" principle. We want to believe we will recognize the Anti-Christ when he makes his appearance and that we will steadfastly refuse his demands. Yet there is a rather uneasy and shameful thought that intrudes on our bravado: will we truly be up to the task?

Scripture tells us the Anti-Christ will be a charismatic leader; an international peacemaker. His arrival at a time of worldwide weariness and global loss of hope will endear him even to the faithful. He will work miracles and be seen as a man blessed with superior, almost supernatural gifts. Distraction will come easily in his powerful presence.

While the Bible tells us this man will become the ambassador of Satan, it will be difficult to make that connection. Why? When? How will we know? *The fact of the matter is we won't.*

In the garden at Gethsemane that night, Jesus found his spirit willing but a body that was weak—a human situation if there ever was one. He begged his Father to reconsider. Perhaps he knew all that would come to pass if we were to be saved; perhaps he did not. Still, amid torture and death, Jesus would remain committed to his Father's will. He purchased our salvation with his bloody death. Knowing in advance or unknowing, it did not make what he went through any easier. It begs the question: how will we fare when our time comes?

Fortunately for us, Jesus gave us the key to that concern in the garden that fateful night. He acceded to his Fathers will. He called on the strength of the Holy Spirit. *He leaned.* What are we to do when our human strength fails us? The very same.

God does not expect us not to be afraid. Fear of death and the unknown is a natural part of being human. Even though in Faith we know there is nothing to fear in dying, it is often thoughts of the process we will go through before he takes us home that haunts us. What price will we be asked to pay before we get there? Will our deaths be full of suffering and pain, will we linger, will we beg for release? Like Jesus in the Garden, our human fears will undoubtedly hijack our own peace from time to time, but we are certainly in good company.

The Bible makes it clear that the end times and the years preceding them will be a very difficult and painful time for humans, believers and unbelievers alike. The very picture the Good Book paints is enough to put terror into the most devout and strong among us. Yet it is the same book Believers must embrace for direction through those confusing times. Choices will be demanded that cannot be avoided.

Even before that day comes, most of us will face our own "end times" as we encounter the deaths of loved ones or our own demise. The dual specters of fear and retribution will surely visit us then. Knowing death can only take us once will be but small comfort. Like Jesus in the Garden, we will pray and plead for respite in our own final days, asking God to deliver us.

Many of us will know death before our own. We will lose loved ones. We will witness suffering from disease. Innocents will pass unfairly. We will ask why. Demand answers. Flail against the Lord in our pain.

We can lean on him, just as his only Son did. We have only to remember that what passes on this earth is but a moment. The Father has promised us eternal joy.

Jesus paid the price for our salvation. No one can take it from us, only we can surrender that gift by refusing to embrace it.

INTERCESSION

When I was a child, Lord, I feared the monster in the closet. He was so real, so predatory and dangerous. What it was about him was unknown, but that made the alarm even worse. The anticipation was dreadful. I did not want to confront whatever it was that terrorized me.

Then, I was alone in an adult world of unbelievers and nay-sayers. All the comforting words of Mom and Dad did not really chase away all the fear, and even leaving the light on, checking out the closet, and pulling the covers over my head didn't settle me much. The unknown monster had control over me, and I was at its mercy.

I know, Lord, that I will face that forever monster: death. This time on earth is a fleeting thing, and this home a temporary one. As a Christian I rejoice in your precious gift of life everlasting. I praise and thank you for the sacrifice of your only Son. Where many unbelievers will lie terrified of the unknown, I have the comforting awareness of what is to come. I've been told, and it is documented in your Book. Death has been defeated for all time! Christ's victory has purchased my eternal life and restored me to my Father's house.

If birth is the first step toward dying, rebirth in Jesus is the final step to life everlasting! For this I give you praise and thanksgiving.

> **Peter 3:10** *The day of the Lord is surely coming, as unexpectedly as thief; and then the heavens will pass away in a terrible noise and the heavenly bodies will disappear in fire and the earth and everything on it will be burned up.*

THE HANGING TREE

My name is Judas Iscariot. I doubt I have to explain myself any further. It's not a common name anymore. Not many parents name their babies after me. In fact, if you look in the dictionary, I wouldn't be surprised to find I am the first definition there for "betrayal." I am the infamous thief who handed over the Son of God with a traitorous kiss to the Synhedrion.

Most people figure I was in it for the money. I sure wasn't thinking about the future or fame at the time I did the thing. I was afraid, and simply trying to find a way out before everything around me collapsed. The money was important because it gave me the means to get away. I was already a thief by nature. Until I met him. Jesus, that is.

When I first became aware of him, he was fast becoming famous in his own right. People were drawn to him despite themselves, just like me. I still can't explain it, but my life changed when I became one of "the Twelve."

We were called his disciples at the time. We travelled with him and we saw some things. Let me tell you, there was wonder in this man. I admired him, truth be told. Except he didn't appear to have any common sense. He couldn't take a hint. The atmosphere of the times, the political intrigue was dangerous enough. Jesus kept mixing it up with the Pharisees anyway, challenging them, embarrassing them publicly, proclaiming himself a king. It's said there's a tenuous line between genius and insanity. I don't know why or when I began to think he'd crossed it, but I surely wasn't the only one.

I mean, it was bound to happen. Somebody was going to end it, probably while ending the rest of us at the same time. Permanently. All I did was take advantage of an opportunity. After all, none of us made a bundle in our time with Jesus. We barely knew from one day to the next where we'd bed down or have supper. When it all came down, we were going to have to run for it, and fast. How were we going to get that done? It would take money and a lot of it to get far enough away until things died down. Maybe none of us could ever return. We sure couldn't start over from scratch somewhere else with no coin. I wasn't anxious to go back to my thieving ways to get by. When there appeared a chance, I took it. It was as simple as that. Leading them to Jesus was only accepting the inevitability of his arrest anyway.

Yeah, I felt bad about it. In a case like this though, it's every man for himself. That's the law of the jungle. If you could just put yourself in my shoes, it's not so hard to figure out. It turned out to be a little more difficult than I expected in the end. I never thought they'd do what they did to him. They told me they were just going to rough him up—pound some sense into him. I knew they wanted—needed—to make an example of him, but crucifixion? I never anticipated that. That really got to me. The guilt ate at me. He was good to me. I never had a problem with him. It got so bad the very thought of those silver pieces became a suffocating weight around my neck-much like the hanging rope I placed there later that day.

I tell you, it wasn't greed.

It was not understanding. God forgive me.

CONTEMPLATION

Let's face it, many of us are suckers for the deal that is too good to be true. We know it's risky, but there is so much to possibly be gained! We gamble a few dollars, overplay our bingo, buy too many lottery tickets, spring for a miracle cure or the latest age-reversing product, an under-the-table stock tip, a sure sports win. We fall for an amazing offer on the internet or a business deal that promises impossible gains. It happens every day in this country, even to those of us who think we are above it all. Ponzi schemes, land deals, investment fraud, product falsifying, illegal gains; there are so many temptations every way we turn.

We seem particularly vulnerable when we are most at risk. When times are tough, we tend to get even more trusting and our justifications more creative. When we're making it check to check, surely God doesn't expect us to tithe more than we can spare? What's wrong with trying to better things for the sake of our family? Strangely enough, some of us who already have so much are as vulnerable to temptation simply because it's never enough. *The Devil plays his same old tune and we dance to his music. We just don't see it that way.*

We are so good at rationalizations. So was Judas. After all, the handwriting was already on the wall. It wasn't his fault that Jesus brought all that on himself. If he didn't take the money, someone else would. Why should he be the one to lose out? Sounds like an echo of Eve's thoughts regarding the forbidden fruit? We forget, temptation is for all time.

When we don't rely on Faith it means we don't trust God. Not trusting and practicing obedience to his will causes us to react with fear and a need to direct our own way. Satan is always on the lookout for that opportunity. His way seldom brings anything but disaster and heartache. On the other hand, Our Lord has promised to take care of his own. Maybe the issue lies in our personal definition of what suffices as needful and necessary?

Jesus didn't try to reason with Judas. His Father didn't stop Judas. God won't stop us. He doesn't label the opportunities we're offered with flashing warning signs and future gleanings of insight. He knows we get the danger. He knows sometimes we want to ignore the implications. He won't gainsay our choices. That was the deal going in. Free will and all that.

So, is your middle name Judas?

There's lots of us who fit the bill, Lord. When you think about it that way, Judas teaches a great lesson. Too often we are so preoccupied with his horrendous deed, we lose sight of the human—the man—and the reasons behind his actions.

The thing is Judas knew remorse; or it's unlikely he'd have hung himself later. If he knew remorse, he must have asked for forgiveness. If he asked for forgiveness, then he was saved—by the very actions of the Man-God he condemned to death.

We can all ask for forgiveness. First, we must have remorse. We must own up to and change our grievous ways—*before the hanging tree comes to call in the guise of the Lords' judgment day.*

INTERCESSION

Judas was a man, Lord. Not so different from any other man. Not so different from me. He was human, so even being male wasn't a condition of his actions. All of us as humans have the same capacity for flawed judgement. It isn't gender specific, by any means. We all have a need to survive. Who knows what we would do to save ourselves and our loved ones from hardship or retribution? Even so, it's rarely a life-or-death decision we're trying to justify.

Have I had opportunities to play the Judas game? Have there been betrayals in my life? Have I taken something I don't deserve or kept something at the cost of another? Have I failed my God, given in to temptation, placed false blame, or rationalized my actions until I succeeded in blinding myself to the truth? Have I judged others, put myself first, or deserted a friend for selfish reasons? Have I placed my own direction above my faith in the Father's plan for me?

I pray that the Father helps me to see it all for what it is. I ask him to shred my false bravado and strip the fig leaves that I cover myself with attempting to hide my secret failings from his eyes.

I repent and ask for God's forgiveness. I will strive from here on to be brutally honest with myself. If I honor God's truth, I can face the temptations that exist all around me for what they are, and not for what I wish them to be.

Give me your strength and keep me close in your ways, Lord. *If I must hide, let it be in Thee.*

> ***Jeremiah 23:23–24*** *Am I a God at hand, declares the* LORD, *and not a God far away? Can a man hide himself in secret places so that I cannot see him? declares the* LORD. *Do I not fill heaven and earth? declares the* LORD.

A SOLDIERS JOURNEY

I'm really just a footnote in history. A witness, so to speak.

I was there that night in the garden. Rousted by my commander in the early morning hours, my unit was given orders to move on a disturbance east of the city. An arrest warrant had been issued for one Jesus of Nazareth and we were to escort him to a holding cell. Our information said his followers were with him. Instructions were to meet any resistance with force, but to bring him back alive.

I'd heard of Jesus, of course. Small town, big rabble rouser. We'd had a few issues regarding crowd control through the months as his popularity grew. There was a lot of political intrigue around him, too. Rumors circulated about black magic and impossible feats of healing and changing water into wine. I'd heard he'd even torn apart a temple not so long ago in a rage about the money lenders there.

The Pharisees were continually baiting him, trying to trick him into admissions of wrongdoing. They wanted him off the streets. The word was this Jesus deftly maneuvered his way around them, causing much public humiliation in the process. Their failure to ensnare him had driven them crazy. It would appear they would finally be getting their revenge tonight. Jesus was to be arrested for treason.

One of his own followers, Judas Iscariot, was to accompany us and identify him. Personally, I found the man distasteful. Anyone with a lack of loyalty always rubbed a soldier, whose life depended on it, the wrong way. Even so, these confidential informants were a necessary evil in our line of work. Hopefully the element of surprise and the quick identification would work in our favor. Maybe we could wrap it up fast and catch some additional sleep before morning call.

Things looked promising when we got there. Most of the group was sleeping or in a daze sitting around a banked fire as we moved in. Immediately, Judas went forward a short distance and kissed Jesus on the cheek. This was the agreed upon signal. The man's followers looked around in confusion, taking in their compatriot's odd behavior and our armed intent. We were all frozen in an uneasy tableau one minute and then in the next, one of his followers took a sword in hand and swiped at me.

The whole thing happened so fast; it didn't seem real. I didn't even feel anything right away. Seconds later I sensed a wet warm liquid running down my neck. Then the pain hit, and I went into shock. In disbelief, I saw my ear lying on the ground. It was such an unexpected blow that everyone was paralyzed for a moment. Then swords were drawn. In slow motion, before it could erupt into a slaughter, this Jesus reached down and picked up my ear. He held it to the side of my neck and the pain instantly stopped. Looking me in the eyes, he healed the wound and bade his disciples to stand down. We arrested him without further incident.

There wasn't much conversation on the way back. All of us were hardened warriors. Not much intimidated us, but what we'd just seen was another matter. If this man could practice black arts-and what other explanation could there be - then would we all be cursed before the night was out for our role in the arrest? When we got back to the barracks, there was little chance of sleep and lots of whispered exchanges and pleas to the gods for protection.

Personally, I didn't have much to say either. I was still overwhelmed, trying to sort it all out. This Jesus healed me. *His enemy*. Why would someone do that? How had he done it? It left me in a place of wonder- and concern.

I knew even before I finally accepted it that my life would not go on as it once was. I had to know more about this man.

It was the beginning of a change; a permanent one.

CONTEMPLATION

We don't know this man's name. There is no follow-up on his life after this experience with the Lord in the Bible.

We do know these were physically violent times. People got hurt and maimed all the time. Punishments were harsh and physically debilitating. Soldiers were used to dispensing cruelty. When it came to having sympathy for the enemy, it just wasn't in a soldier's make up. The disciples were in a quandary too. Why did Jesus tell them to stand down? They were willing to battle in his defense, to protect him and spirit him away even if it cost them their lives.

Did Jesus act as he did because this arrest was necessary to set the final stage for his last earthly journey in motion? Was he protecting his beloved disciples from slaughter at the hands of an enraged militia? Or making sure his followers would live to preach his word after his death? Was it because he was a pacifist by nature and abhorred violence? Probably all of it, and more.

It was a confusing time all around. It would be naïve to suggest that the events didn't touch everyone involved that fateful night. A contact with Christ was not one that left you unchanged.

While we have the story about the disciples and how their lives were affected after this incident in the garden, we don't know anything about the healed soldier, or his comrades. Without doubt, some of them tried to put the incident away from them as soon as possible, dismissing the whole matter. The belief in the dark magics common to the times did not encourage exploration.

It seems likely the soldier who benefited directly from the Lord's intervention had a much harder time going back to business as usual? Could Jesus heal anyone physically without healing him spiritually as well? Is there something key here besides a miracle and the effect on a Centurion?

Jesus was always about the message. If we look closely, he remained so right up through those last days. *Maybe his actions from the moment of his arrest forward were for our benefit as well as for the completion of his ordained mission.*

Throughout the days of torture and death that would come on the heels of that fateful night, Jesus would remain implacably peaceful and patiently forgiving; filled with compassion and healing right up to the end.

He healed the soldier first. He begged his Father even in his extremis to forgive those who participated in his death, suggesting that "they know not what they do". With his last breath he forgave a common criminal, taking the man with him into his Father's kingdom.

Perhaps Jesus practiced what he preached? Perhaps he preached best by example?

CONTEMPLATION

Father help me to put into daily practice the virtues that embodied Jesus in his time on this earth. He taught by example and I would do the same. I would live in peace and offer peace to those who challenge my ways. I would forgive and seek forgiveness; to offer healing to those in spiritual and physical need, to serve as a beacon of hope to those unsure of the way.

As a committed Believer, I am secure in the belief that only in Christ can I triumph over diversity and in doing so, touch others with the wonder of God's love and acceptance.

May I follow Christ's example, and lead by my own in his name.

Peter 2:21 For to this you have been called, because Christ also suffered for you, leaving you as an example so that you might follow in his steps.

PILATE THE POWERLESS

His palms were sweaty.

Fastidious to a fault, Pontius hated that clammy, moist feeling of perspiration coating his hands. No matter how often he washed them, it did no good. It was stress, of course. What else? The high priest at his right, the rabble-rouser Jesus at his left, Rome and Syria watching with unabated interest. It was a tense situation with a lot at stake. He knew the Sanhedrin had instigated these charges against the Nazarene. They were, by Roman authority, the governing body of Jerusalem. Pontius Pilate's authority was frustratingly limited in some respects, and he felt it keenly in this situation. He walked a proverbial tightrope, trying to keep Rome's interests foremost while not antagonizing the Jews, who heartily resented Roman rule. Keeping a balance between the two factions while keeping himself in a favorable position was a constant challenge. After all, he was an ambitious man. Nothing wrong with that. He was destined for much greater things than Jerusalem had to offer. Pontius was also aware that if things got out of hand, Syria would descend on the city with its large army to put down any hint of revolt. That would not look good for him.

Personally, he didn't have any problem with this man, Jesus, but the pressure to convict him was intense. Disciplining himself, he resisted an overwhelming urge to wipe his hands on his tunic. Beads of sweat began to pop out on his forehead, and he could feel moisture dripping down the back of his neck. He sensed the malicious stare of the high priest. Being very careful to show no weakness or concern, he moved to the open balcony. Not even the slightest breeze moved the air to cool his troubled spirit—it was like the air itself held its breath.

And this Jesus. This "King of the Jews." Didn't he know to proclaim himself king of anything was treason of the worst kind? Then he'd been baiting the Pharisees for months on end. Pontius couldn't say he hadn't enjoyed that some. As for the kingdom, let the man rave on about it. It didn't intimidate him in the least. Certainly, these were minor issues. The man was not deserving of severe punishment.

Pontius flinched when he thought about how he'd sent Jesus to Herod for judgment. Even though Jesus was Galilean and technically under Pilate's jurisdiction, Herod was the Prefect of all Judea. Herod was no dummy, though. He'd sent Jesus back. He couldn't get much out of him, either and while he didn't really feel the charges sufficient to condemn the man, he wasn't going to put his head in a political noose. He'd rather Pontius did that.

He studied Jesus again. You had to admit, the Nazarene was one cool customer. He seemed almost resigned—like he already knew the outcome. Didn't he get it? Pontius was his only possible deliverer. This disinterested manner made

Pontius angry and—curiously—afraid. It wasn't like he hadn't tried. He'd really given the man every out. Point blank he'd asked him, not once but several times, "Are you the King of the Jews?"

"As you say it," he'd replied.

What kind of an answer was that? It irritated him. Yet when he looked again into the quiet, untroubled eyes of this peasant from Galilee, it was a distasteful duty he faced.

It was almost like he feels sorry for me. *Like he knows something I don't know,* Pontius thought to himself. It was very unsettling. On the other hand, why should he care? Glancing once again at the prisoner, Pontius couldn't help but notice that Jesus seemed to grow calmer as Pontius grew less at ease. It made his skin crawl. Jesus was certainly unprepossessing in manner and bearing. Just how much of a threat could he be? Of course, the rumors were preposterous. Miracles, indeed. There must be a way ... got it! His spirits immediately lifted with a possible solution. One that would effectively take him out of the equation without alienating the High Priests. With the celebration of Passover, he was permitted to release one prisoner. He would bring out Barabbas, the notorious murderer who had just recently been arrested. He would afford his people their choice between the Nazarene and the reviled Barabbas. No way would the people let Barabbas go. There was a real criminal.

The feral scent of the restless crowd carried up to the balcony in the suffocating, expectant air. Before he stepped outside to announce his decision, Pontius called again for a basin and washed his hands one more time. Returning to the veranda, he spoke thus: "Good people of Jerusalem, I have given much thought to the situation at hand. On this auspicious day, the law permits us to free a prisoner. I offer to you, my loyal subjects, the very choice of whom that will be: this Jesus of Galilee or the murdering thief Barabbas. You will decide who shall go free and who of these two shall be condemned to death."

Then it began—quietly at first. Incredulously, Pontius Pilate listened as the crowd began to chant with increasing fervor, "Crucify the Nazarene!" He could see the figures moving among the people, stirring up the crowd, urging them to a greater frenzy until the roar for Jesus' crucifixion was all that could be heard.

Pontius Pilate was dumbfounded. How could this be? Had not he given them a choice that seemed clear cut? He could not gainsay the crowd now and was desperate to get back inside. In the end, what was it to him? This was a peasant, a rabble-rouser, and a man technically guilty of treason. There was no culpability here; the man had condemned himself by his own words. Herod had sent Jesus back already flogged and beaten. Now Pontius Pilate presented Jesus to the guards for crucifixion. Two thieves had been hanged at Golgotha earlier. Before the day was out, the Nazarene would join them. He was done with the entire matter and retired to the comfort of his living quarters.

Unconsciously, out of sight of the crowd, he wiped his hands repeatedly on his tunic. He could not get them dry. He could not get them clean.

Somehow, he knew that nothing would ever make them clean again.

CONTEMPLATION

Pontius Pilate was not a sensitive man by nature. If he was oddly troubled that day, it was because no one Christ met came away untouched. That meeting with Jesus left him confused, angry, and irritated. Yet despite a clear reluctance, he went along with the conspiracy to kill Jesus. While the prophesies of ancient times had to be fulfilled, could Pilate have refused to pass sentence anyway?

We humans can always choose against the majority, but we are not likely to do so. More importantly, there would be key players in history for the Scriptures to be fulfilled, and one of them was Pontius Pilate. Such a trespass, though. Could even God forgive it? Did Pilate even seek forgiveness?

We do not know the outcome. None of us knows for sure what the long-term impact was that Jesus had on Pontius or what was in his heart by the end of his lifetime. We do know that God gives us all more than one opportunity to choose him. Still, Pontius is only one of the "losers" in the Bible that we are relieved was not us.

Was he really that different from you and me though? We've all found ourselves in dicey situations, wanting to do the right thing, but reluctant to go against the majority. It happens to individuals, to companies, to nations. Outside interests can bring tremendous pressure to bear, and peers insist on our complicity. We might not agree with what is going on. We might not be comfortable, but will our faith prove strong enough to resist surrender? To stand alone for truth, if we must? If we're honest, it's just easier sometimes to go along or to give in, or at the very least to keep our mouths shut. It's a human weakness the devil appreciates.

Some of the greatest conspiracies in history were implemented by single individuals with the power to persuade other men into reluctant followers. From a bully who recruits a gang around him to a political shaker who embroils others in a secret plot, power corrupts. More importantly, anyone who wields it is vulnerable to its possession.

Power thrives on contradiction. There is always too much of it, or too little. It is coveted or resented, bestowed, or withheld. It manipulates or dictates, controls, and defies—and many times, it is all done in the name of the greater good. Certainly, the temptations that come with it are the devil's favorite playground. When Satan had his choice of what to tempt a weakened, fasting Christ with, out of all the choices he might have made, he chose the gift of absolute power in the guise of dominion over all the cities of the world. He is still at work today, and the prize is curiously the same: world domination. He's working the same track because it's so successful. The sin of Eden, the first sin, was a choice for power, and so it has been since. That is why Christ's temptation was even necessary: Jesus had to show the defeat of power's vast temptations can be realized with him as our guide.

We must pray for those who walk with power, who must trod this dangerous, slippery slope. We are all at risk for the consequences.

Because the Devil always comes ... rejoicing.

First and foremost, he is an opportunist.

INTERCESSION

Help me, Lord, to use the power you have gifted me with in this lifetime for your glory. Whether I am a teacher, a community leader, or a city enforcer - the head of a family, company, or team - you have given me the power to lead. I need your help to be ever vigilant for the human weaknesses so easily exploited in its tempting embrace. Make me always aware my use of or misuse of power impacts all those around me. My actions as a leader make those who follow me vulnerable to my choices, as well.

Only you can fully appreciate the truth of power and the machinations of how readily it corrupts. It is a sly and false prophet, easily accepted in its many disguises and as varied as temptation can be.

Protect and safeguard our leaders of every kind from self-deceit, self-aggrandizement, and greed. We pray for them all. Not even the least among them is exempt from our heartfelt concern, for only you can open their eyes to see and their hearts to true discernment.

Help us to stand strong in our own leadership, and when we are called to stand in our Faith, even as we stand out from others, give us the courage of your Holy Spirit to act in your name.

For surely whoever shall misuse your power from the lowliest to the most exalted will be held accountable even as Lucifer was, and whoever you give power to lead will be held to an even stronger accounting.

> **Peter 5:2–3** *Shepherd the flock of God among you, exercising oversight not under compulsion, but voluntarily, according to the will of God and not for sordid gain, but with eagerness, nor yet as lording it over those allotted to your charge, but proving to be examples to the flock.*

THE GUY ON THE LEFT

To this day few know my name.

I was the "bad thief" (as opposed to that guy on my right, I guess). We'll call him the "good thief, even if in my opinion, the only good thief is a free one. That day on Calvary pretty much summed up my luck. The Pharisees of course, had their own point of view: all thieves were deserving of death -an equal treatment for one and all policy.

You could say I was just hanging around (no pun intended) when a crowd approached the hill that day. A bloodied man staggered under the load of a heavy cross. He was badly beaten, with more blood pouring from open wounds on his head. What a mess. Somebody sure had it in for him.

The merciless whips of the Praetorian Guard bullied him into a place between us. I watched as they stripped him and laid him on the rough-hewn cross. They took stakes and pounded them through his wrists and ankles.

My fellow lawbreaker and I were bound with ropes that held us fast, causing us to slump painfully. Eventually, we would no longer be able to hold ourselves up. We were meant to die a death of torturous muscle spasms, dehydration, and starvation. Bad enough by anyone's standards, but this man's offence must be great. The manner of his execution was extreme, and his death was sure to be the same. I winced as the nails split his flesh. From a purely selfish point of view, things were tough enough around here. I found myself wishing they'd hang him somewhere else.

That sign: "Jesus, King of the Jews." Familiar. I'd heard of the man. Well, that changed things. Not too smart, proclaiming himself king in these uncertain times. I never had much schooling myself, but even I could figure that one out. He'd been going around, bragging about his treason in public, too. Must be missing more than a few sesterces, that one. Bringing the crowds all around, challenging the Pharisees left and right was hardly smart. What'd he think—that he was untouchable?

Sure, I'd heard his rambling toward the end. All that malarkey about another life, forgiveness, and all that rubbish. Life is hell, and then you die. If you ask me, one time around is misery enough. Can't think of a worse nightmare than having to live it all over again.

What was that? That other guy on the right—what was he saying to this King of Jews? He must be out of his mind with delirium, to believe this Jesus was going home, much less taking anyone with him? I heard Jesus forgive him. He even told him he'd be with him at his right hand.

Whatever gets you through, I guess. More like it, he'd lie in a common grave on Potter's Hill with the rest of us. Death: the great equalizer. The king and the paupers, lain together Fact is, you come into this world alone, and you leave it alone. Then, him calling on his dad. Proof right there. Like his dad could be of any help. My old man threw me out when I was barely old enough to panhandle on the temple steps. Set me up on my career path, you might say. Still, it was easy to start imagining all sorts of crazy things; just wanting to believe, wanting it to be over.

He spoke to me, too, you know. He even called me by my name, Dismas. For just a moment, I thought I saw him in glorious splendor. He put his hand out to me …

CONTEMPLATION

Are you one of those people who believe there is always more time? Are you a doubting Thomas, waiting for proof? Or a tough guy? That's your story, and you're sticking to it? If you're a real cynic—you've seen it all, and you're not going to be had—then you've got a lot in common with the guy on the left. He wasn't going to be anybody's fool, either.

Under the dire circumstances, just in case this Jesus was on the level, it might have made more sense for Dismas to take the chance and get on board before it was too late. In denial right up until the end, he just didn't seem able to change the patterns of a lifetime. He was fortunate, though. He got the chance.

The truth is with the first beat of our hearts, we are already moving toward death. Every day, we walk a dangerous precipice. Human beings are notorious for thinking they're indestructible or that they won't be the one taken by surprise when death comes calling. Particularly when we are young and healthy, we forget the world around us isn't tuned into our reality. Lives are snuffed out every day by mistakes, disease, accidents, and another's impact on our world. We clearly aren't in control. For many of us, death will come out of the blue. There will be no time to reach out, to say that Act of Contrition we've been saving up. It's not wise, holding onto our ticket to ride until the proverbial horse has left the gate.

Live your life anticipating your death. It's the one sure thing you can count on in this world.

Live ready, and you'll be ready.

INTERCESSION

Help me, Lord, to stay in a state of readiness so that I may receive your grace and everlasting life when the time comes. Procrastination isn't the wise choice here. That guy on the left couldn't have been thinking too clearly. He waited too long to surrender to Jesus—or maybe he did with his last breath? We'll never know. Second-guessing is not a comfortable place to be. I don't want my loved ones second guessing my choices when they have to let me go.

I pray, Father, that you will remind me daily in your wisdom to keep my heart and mind focused on the path I walk, the path that leads to you. That way, you are always in my present, and I don't have to worry about cutting it too close. *The only fool I want to be is a fool for your love, Lord.*

Romans 13:11–14 *Besides this you know the time, that the hour has come for you to wake* *from sleep. For salvation is nearer to us now than when we first believed. The night is far gone; the day is at hand. So then let us cast off the works of darkness and put on the armor of light. Let us walk properly as in the daytime, not in orgies and drunkenness, not in sexual immorality and sensuality, not in quarreling and jealousy. But put on the Lord, Jesus, Christ, and make no provision for the flesh, to gratify its desires.*

A FOOL FOR LOVE

They spat on him. Stripping his garments, they shamed him. They beat him and gave him a crown of thorns as they bowed down before him. Fashioning a crude cross of wood, they set him on his way through the crowded thoroughfare of the city, weak, bleeding, and driven before them like an animal.

He did not fight back. He did not protest or resist. He did not try to vindicate himself nor did he insist on his innocence. Undoubtedly his pathetic dignity drove his captors to an even greater frenzy of cruelty, like men are when caught up in a blood lust that takes all reason and accountability from them.

It was not the first time he had behaved oddly. On the last Passover, he'd washed the ffeet of the twelve. Kneeling before them the self -professed "Son of God" bent himself to the task of menial service. He cradled those dirty, sweaty, travel-stained feet, callused and torn from harsh roads and dusty by-ways with gentle hands.

How confused and uncomfortable the apostles must have been! Embarrassed and incredulous, it was perhaps not the first time they had felt so. Sheepishly glancing at one another, silently questioning each other; was the man they served not, at times, a little mad?

There was that occasion when he intervened in the punishment of a common prostitute. It was not fitting. He touched the lepers, the unspeakable outcasts, and the destitute of God. He healed the profane and the sick by laying his very own hands upon them. For all they were proud to do his bidding, there were surely times even they were left feeling foolish by his actions.

Men feeling foolish are often men sorely afraid. When times got tough, they slunk away and melted into the unforgiving landscape. One of them, at a cock's crow collapsing in a paradox of agony composed of equal parts grief and denial. Another skulking off with forty pieces of silver weighing heavily on him, feeling not like the reprieve he'd imagined, but a certain call to death.

Then. when they suspended Jesus on the cross, proclaiming him the King of the Jews and he died there, in the ignoble company of two common thieves, it was a final blow. He did not save himself. His father did not spare him. So, on the heels of his foolish surrender came the overwhelming fear: maybe they were the biggest fools of all.

CONTEMPLATION

Jesus' death was undoubtedly a terrible dilemma for his disciples. In their experience, dead was dead. Whatever they'd hoped, it was easier to believe in his message and promises when Jesus was alive. Even though their master had tried to prepare them, asking human beings to grasp what was impossible to them did not seem to carry much weight after the fact. Cowering and in fear of their lives, they must have felt totally bewildered. They probably felt betrayed and humiliated as well. Of course, the Scriptures had predicted Jesus' victory over death and the disciples had heard it from Jesus himself, but I doubt that was the first thing on their minds that day on the hill. The three days after, before the Lord rose in victory, must have seemed an eternity away.

While Jesus knew the Old Testament had to be fulfilled, in the interim it was an impossible place for his disciples to be left. Ill-equipped to begin preaching his Word, the mute and terrified followers simply cowered together after Jesus' death, probably waiting for their own deaths and retaliation in the guise of the dreaded knock on the door.

Then he showed up. Can we even imagine the feeling?

The disciples and other faithful followers were the first to see the resurrected Jesus. They were privileged and blessed by the Lord. When the Holy Spirit gave them the eloquent speech of many tongues, the fire of their zeal was upon them. God did not forsake them. He sent his resurrected Son and the Spirit of his love to make the impossible possible. He will do it again.

INTERCESSION

I know you understand my weaknesses and my fears, Lord. I know you have provided me with your Word and your beloved Holy Spirit to give me the strength to do your will.

Still, how I wish sometimes that I had been one of the witnesses of that earlier time; the one to see you and to place my hands in your wounds as once Thomas did. It would be so much easier.

Of course, then it would be easy for us all. I am sure it was not so for the disciples even after your return. In fact, many of them would die martyrs' deaths in the pursuit of your will. Their task was difficult, and the first of its kind. They deserved the gifts the Father gave them.

In truth, each one of us could become one of those who, once struck dumb in the discovery of the Father's love soon find their tongues running away with them whether they will it or no. We could find ourselves unable to contain our exuberance. The Holy Spirit is alive and well in our own times! We have but to open our hearts to him. Yet, our own uncertainties, our reservations about appearing fools keeps us from letting go, So, Lord, give us cowardly beings the same gift of gab that your Holy Spirit bestowed on those fearful disciples that day. Help us to open our hearts and to dismiss our pride, to go forth in witness and to proclaim your glory for now and forever.

Isaiah 41:10 Fear not for I am with you. Do not look around in terror and be dismayed, for I am your god. I will strength and harden you, I will hold you up and retain you with my victorious right hand of rightness and justice.

MARY OF SORROWS

She cradled him gently in her arms as once she'd held him on the night of his birth so long ago. Then her heart had never known such joy. Holding the beaten, bruised shell of her son Jesus close to her heart now, she sobbed in grief and despair. Her faith in his message was unshakeable, but it was her Mother's heart that ached with the loss. She was grateful his suffering had finally ended. Still, her humanity struggled with the knowledge that she would never hold him again, never touch his hand or experience the twinkle of humor in his eyes. She bent now to gently wipe the bloodied stains from his brow. As she crooned the lullaby of ancient loss, she thought back.

On that clear, cold night so very long ago she had rocked him in wonder, keeping him warm, safe, and protected. While her heart overflowed with love, she'd marveled again how the Father had seen her worthy to bring this savior child into the world. All she'd had to offer was her faith in a vision.

Soon now she would swaddle him one last time, anointing him with the same gifts of frankincense and myrrh that marked his entrance into this world. It was curiously fitting somehow that while he had been born into a stranger's stable, he would be laid to rest in another's donated tomb. All that was once of

Jesus was the love and the message he would leave behind. Would it be enough? In her grief, she searched his face, looking for the answers.

He would have chided her for her lack of faith. She smiled. His features so peacefully at rest resembled nothing of the man or the son. The mischievous eyes of the twelve-year-old that stole away to the temple to do his Father's work were weary and hollow. The warm, penetrating gaze of the compassionate healer no longer burned. His hands, long and slender, hung limply, covered in blood that was now clotted and black; his head bruised and punctured by the cruel thorns pressing even now on his gaunt skull.

She was a foolish old woman. This was not her son. If the truth be told, he had never been hers. He was born to this destiny; he had told her often enough. As a man, she knew his work on earth was done and glad she was of it. His pain was her pain and no more could be born.

Long ago, when she was told by an angel that she would bear this King of Kings, she had bowed her head. She had played her part, responding "Thy will be done." And so, it had been.

Placing a final kiss upon his brow, Mary commended him to his heavenly Father, bowing her head in prayer and acceptance. Reluctantly, she stood and began the long walk back to town.

CONTEMPLATION

To lose a child is a permanent blight upon the soul. To watch a child suffer, to be helpless to change it is heart-wrenching. Any parent who has experienced that intimate loss will tell you it's true: it is unnatural to outlive your progeny. Most would give their own lives to prevent it.

Even as an adult, those born of your loins remain your children. When they are hurt, you hurt. When they struggle, you suffer. When they die, a little piece of you is gone as well.

Mary lived her whole life knowing her son was about God's work. Her understanding of what that role entailed was one that probably grew with experience. She likely never had foreknowledge of his cruel death, but like most mothers, she must have worried about what his mission demanded of him. As he made himself more and more conspicuous, concerns about possible retribution no doubt cost her many sleepless nights. Where are the words to describe her suffering while her Son languished on the cross? To look upon that tortured face? To suffer his agony in her own heart? Surely that vision would have remained with her the rest of her life had not the Father showed mercy. She couldn't have known that moment the news of a Risen Christ would transcend the agony of that burning torment, replacing it for all time with the reality of a Man-God risen in all his glory. Yet to experience that blessing, when Mary held Jesus in her arms for the last time, did her faith falter? Who could blame her?

Perhaps Mary, already acquainted with angels and an Immaculate Conception, had the comfort of her unique experiences to anchor her in that terrible moment. She believed in God's plan because she was directly a part of it. Unbelievable things had happened to her from the time she was a girl. It's possible God gave her extra helpings of grace in her time of need, until the visible proof of a Risen Christ could grant her the eternal comfort she deserved.

Regardless, it was a devastating time. Was she alone? Where was Joseph? What happened to Mary afterward? The Bible doesn't see fit to give us those details. Perhaps they are unnecessary to the message or our need. What is important is the mother of God paid a terrible price, as many of us have. She was a fully human being, and the tearing she felt was no different than our own.

The only comfort she, and we, can take is in the Lords promises. Our loved ones are never lost to us. In time, we will all be reunited. The scales will be lifted from our eyes and we will see the vision the Almighty has created.

Until then, we will grieve, as Mary did, even in our acceptance of God's will. We will pray for comfort and find reassurance in his word. For did the Father not share in our grief with the death of his own Son? He knows us. We belonged to him first. In him we will all be united and know eternal peace.

INTERCESSION

Dear Lord, there are times in my life when I don't think I want to survive. Some things are just too hard for humans to bear. There is anger and denial. I rage against you. I ask where is the compassion, the love? How could you do this to me or mine? I feel abandoned. I feel betrayed. Wanting my faith to be strong enough to ease my loss does not make it so. Trying to keep in mind your grand design seems an exercise in futility. It's just too easy to forget this earth is only a temporary home, regardless of your teachings.

I can only ask for your forgiveness, Father, for being short-sighted in my human grief. You gave me the ability to love, to feel, to know devastating loss. This tapestry of life you weave is not one I can easily decipher. Unexpected things happen, and the entwining, colorful threads I want to visualize as a blessed and beautiful work-in-progress suddenly pale with the horror of change. I know though, Father, that you hold the completed work in your loving hands. The finished pattern is yours to know.

Cradle my hurting heart, Lord, and help me in faith to know that all will be well. Make the story we weave together prove worthy of your plan. Give me the vision to recognize it as my own and to put myself in your capable hands, yielding to your promise of life everlasting. Amen.

Revelation 21:4 He will wipe every tear from their eyes. There will be no more death or mourning or crying or pain, for the old order of things has passed away.

THOMAS THE DOUBTFUL

What was the world coming to? The Master gone, laid in a tomb like any mortal man. Every one of them in fear of his life, feeling foolish and a little betrayed.

Well, what did any of them expect? He should have known better. He'd always prided himself on his cautious ways and reserved manner. Thomas spoke little, but he saw much. There were so many fools in this world.

Now, to his chagrin, he was one of them. Skulking in the shadows, avoiding the light of day. Afraid of his own shadow. Not until Jesus had come along did he ever recall feeling anything but sure of himself. It wasn't his most endearing quality and had got him into more than one fix. Arrogant, people called him. Opinionated and bull-headed. Had to know everything for himself. And what was wrong with that he asked?

Now, here they were, trying to tell him Jesus had risen from the dead. He wasn't going for it. Not again. It was mass hysteria, that's all it was. Unless he could put his fingers into the nail wound in Jesus' palms and place his hand into the lanced side of the man, he was for his old ways: let reality be proof positive.

He'd been there when they'd taken down the battered, limp body of Jesus that day. There was nothing in that moment that showed him any different from any other human remains. He hadn't saved himself. Nor had his so-called Father in heaven. He hadn't healed his own wounds. He had even cried out like any man at the end. The jig was up.

In fact, Thomas was thinking that maybe he should just sort of fade away. Hanging all together like this was risky. There was nothing to be gained by staying around here when all was now seen for what it was. He'd head out somewhere new, where there was no chance he'd be identified as one of the Twelve. Didn't the rest realize that congregating in one room like this made them all sitting ducks?

He'd join them one last time—just to say good-bye. He owed them that much. Then he'd leave them as he'd found them: pathetic, wounded, and lost. They just hadn't figured it all out yet.

CONTEMPLATION

Man is a sensory animal by nature. It's how we have survived as a species. We understand our reality based on what we can see, touch, hear, feel, and taste. You're asking a lot of us to take anything on pure Faith. It goes against our very natures.

Taking all that into account, you can't judge Thomas too harshly. He was human like the rest of us. Under the circumstances and given his own personality, which among us might not have felt the same? Considering what all the disciples had just been through, Thomas had reason to question their sanity. It was expected with all that had happened. They were afraid for their very lives.

Still, Thomas got lucky. He made that last get-together and the Lord appeared again. He insisted on giving Thomas the proof he needed to believe. How must Thomas have felt? Ashamed, miserable, embarrassed, incredulous? Blessed? None of us would have that privilege in our lifetime.

Jesus knew there would be a lot of Thomas in many of us. He understood our human natures. He most certainly appeared after his death to fulfill the prophesies, but he came as well to strengthen his followers, so all who came after would know his message. His disciples needed the gift of an emissary who would remain with them through the trying times ahead. They needed confirmation of a miracle. Jesus knew he would overcome their paralyzing fear with the anointing of the Holy Spirit so they could begin the work he had groomed them for. Even Thomas.

While we all live in a world of skepticism, we don't have to be a doubting Thomas. As Christians, we are more blessed than those who lived in Thomas' time. Look how common-place the impossible and the invisible have become in our times!

Everywhere we look, every day there are discoveries of new incredible realities for us to digest and celebrate. Those findings are only the detection of truths that have been there all along. It should be even easier for us to accept as common place things we do not understand and believe in today. Isn't that exactly what an act of faith is?

Maybe God is preparing those of us living in the here and now to rely less on ourselves and more on his Truth? Each new awareness of a magnificent mystery unveiled challenges us, even without the advantages of Thomas, to justify our trust in the Creator. *A true artist can't help but show himself in his Masterpiece.* The Father is revealing himself to us in his created work here on earth. With each new discovery in our world, we come to know him more intimately.

As fast as we are doing the impossible, it's hard not to get it. Truth is only the impossible revealed. God is no less.

INTERCESSION

Lord, it's difficult for any of us to take a leap off a cliff; even if someone we love and trust tells us he is there, waiting to catch us. It's obviously in us to do it, though: look at today's extreme sports. Consider man in space, walking on the moon and docking with space stations. We might not believe it, but the drive to excel and exceed and to do the impossible is obviously somewhere in our DNA!

Of course, I'm not one of those people, Lord. Am I?

I guess your words on that day to Thomas were a message to all future generations: life is about accepting the impossible and getting past it. It's about growing, reaching, and striving beyond the limits we place on ourselves. We've all been there, and sometimes we're amazed at what we can do in our everyday lives if we must.

With the gift of your Holy Spirit, we believers are today's super-charged heroes. We are called upon to share our vision, to thrive on the unknown forces of God in our daily existence. Our daring in doing so is meant to inspire others to be unafraid, to trust their hearts.

It may not be easy to be a Christian in today's world, but has it ever been any different? It has always been necessary for Believers to stand up, to be seen and counted proudly in this contrary world, whatever the costs. Many have paid dearly for the privilege. I ask in the name of your Holy Spirit that you impart to me the strength and courage to take that leap into your waiting arms, and to being everyone I can with me. My faith made visible speaks your word to all, and your word brings all of us salvation Give me wings, Lord, and I will fly!

> **Peter 1:8–9** *Though you have not seen him, you love him and even though you do not see him now, you believe in him and are filled with an inexpressive and glorious joy, for you are receiving the end of your faith, the salvation of your souls.*

THE GOD-MAN
CONUNDRUM

Surely, some of us have asked ourselves if Jesus could have been fully human in the fullest sense of the word.

After all, he fasted forty days and forty nights. It's been done, but it's not something readily embraced. He never married, never had children. Not unheard of ... but most humans choose differently. His job—well let's face it, he pretty much set his own hours. He took his shelter where it was offered and his meals pretty much the same. Seems like a pretty casual style of living; relying on the generosity of others. Of course, it's not like that hasn't been done before either.

He wasn't naïve, exactly. He did turn down an offer few men could refuse: dominion over all the cities of the world, all the riches of the earth. Of course, some might suggest he was lacking in common sense, even a little bit reckless. Others might have thought he had a secret death wish.

Jesus sure didn't know how to back off. He was all about the Message. You might say he was an in-your-face kind of guy, not so much an offensive type to most (the Pharisees excepted), but surely direct and insistent. He could make you uncomfortable and unsure of yourself. Then, he did things the way they weren't supposed to be done: eating with the beggars, preaching to thieves and prostitutes and spending his company with all manner of unsavory sorts. He surely wasn't concerned about catering to those who could wield influence on his behalf!

A common carpenter, the people he surrounded himself with and called disciples were men who eked out a living in their own trades. They worked hard and stank of the fish they caught and the sea. Their clothes were tattered, and their ways rough. Their feet were dirty and torn, hands blistered and callused. They were not the elite, the well-dressed, the pleasant-smelling members of society.

Jesus had simply called them, and they had followed. Most of them still hadn't figured out just how it happened in the first place. Maybe they felt it couldn't hurt. Maybe they were just fed up, angry and discouraged because of the political climate of the time. Could be Jesus' teachings resonated with them as a new way to fight back. Surely, they had to grow from whatever that first reason was into the reality of what Christ was about? I doubt all their wives and families and neighbors were convinced of their choices, either. *Fishers of men, he said. Well, they all still had to eat.*

CONTEMPLATION

How many human beings throughout the ages have entertained the thought that expecting us to follow in the way of the Lord Jesus is asking just a little too much of our mere mortal natures? We cannot free our heads of the notion that being the Son of God, Jesus must have had an easier time of it. Being divine as well as human, he surely had extra help. How then can our Father expect us to live to up to the same standards? It seems a little unfair.

Was Jesus truly human?

He had a mother, Mary. Mothers are something we share in kind. His growing up years must have been awkward for Mary, full of worrying and trying times—like his adventure in the temple at thirteen. We know Jesus chastised his mother for being so concerned. Sounds like a typical teenager to me! Surely that was not the only incident? Think how the young man Jesus felt when he was helpless to protect his mother as she suffered unbearably at his harrowing death? Most of us would spare our mothers' suffering at all costs.

He knew betrayal too, and that by a trusted friend. Who doesn't know those feelings: anger, resentment, sorrow, confusion, despair? Family betrayals are the worst. Like most of us, he experienced feelings of abandonment when the chips were down and people he loved denied any association with him. Been there, done that. Everybody's on board when things are going great, but let suspicion or rumor raise its damning head and you can count your friends, and sometimes your family, on your thumbs.

The demands on Jesus! Constant was the criticism of his every move. Those who followed him expected everything from him: healing, instruction, food, political salvation, and the promises of the Scriptures of old. It surely must have been exhausting. No escape from the crowds, the ill, the needy or the hostile. Mothers and Dads know the same kinds of overwhelming demands raising the children who depend on them.

Then, he was brought into the world poor materially. Born into a lowly manger. Raised as a carpenter's son. His almighty Father did not lift a finger to ease his martyrdom or excuse his death. He left the same way he came in: born and buried in borrowed spaces donated by others. Wouldn't his message have been better received if his material wealth had been more?

He was rich in other ways we can relate to: his family, friends and his work. Surely, he knew laughter and the camaraderie of people who believed in him and shared his daily life?

Still, he travelled on foot, went hungry, was sorely afraid. Obviously, things could have been much easier for him, but could that be where the necessity of being truly and fully human really comes in?

Jesus was blessed with friendship, joy and family. Love, laughter and purpose filled his days. On the other hand, he was not protected from human pain, betrayal, hardship or loss. He was misunderstood, dismissed, humiliated, hunted, harassed, unappreciated, used, shamed, betrayed, hurt, and judged. In the end, these are the things that prevailed and lead to a final, unfair and cruel death at a young age.

If he was indeed blessed with more than the rest of us, then his life surely took more from him than it should have? In that sense, if we could justify his way as being too hard, even unrealistic for us to follow, we 'd be off the hook. We could feel vindicated, easily rationalizing it wasn't reasonable or fair. But his humanness strikes a clear note in our hearts. We have all shared the human experiences he knew.

Maybe Jesus was a God-man for a simple reason: so no human could use his being the Son of God as an excuse for not being strong enough to follow in his ways?

Pick up your cross and follow him. After all, he carried the weight of humanity—and you, on his.

> **Mark 8:34–37** *And He summoned the crowd with His disciples, and said to them, "If anyone wishes to come after Me, he must deny himself, and take up his cross and follow Me. For whoever wishes to save his life will lose it, but whoever loses his life for My sake and the gospel's will save it. For what does it profit a man to gain the whole world, and forfeit his soul?"*

CPSIA information can be obtained
at www.ICGtesting.com
Printed in the USA
FSHW011527210520
70469FS